Roping the Wind

Roping the Wind

A Personal History
of
Cowboys and the Land

Lyman Hafen

Utah State University Press
Logan, Utah
1995

Cover painting in watercolor by Roland Lee. Used by permission.
Lines from "It's Been a Long Time, Pardner" are from *Echoes of the Past: the Cowboy Poetry of Melvin Whipple.* Copyright © 1987 The University of Texas Institute of Texan Cultures at San Antonio. Used by permission.

Utah State University Press
Logan, UT 84322–7800

Typography by WolfPack

Cover design by Holly Broome-Hyer

Library of Congress Cataloging-in-Publication Data

Hafen, Lyman.
    Roping the wind : a personal history of cowboys and the land /
Lyman Hafen.
        ISBN 0-87421-188-3
            p. cm.
        1. Hafen, Lyman. 2. Cowboys—West (U.S.)—Biography.   I. Title.
F596.H23 1995
979'.03'088636—dc20   95–4341
                                                                       CIP

THIS BOOK IS dedicated to my uncles Eldon and Herschel Hafen, and to my father, Kelton Hafen—originators of the ∃Ҡ outfit. And to all the blackbrush cowboys who are still making a go of it.

Acknowledgments

PORTIONS OF THIS book have appeared, in slightly different form, in *St. George Magazine, Nevada Magazine, Tailwind, Northern Lights,* and *In the Shade of the Cottonwoods: Notes on a Small-Town Boyhood.*

Thanks to Bill Holm who first suggested this as a publishable project, to Dorothy Solomon and Ed Lueders for their encouragement and advice, to Edward Geary for his valuable suggestions, and to Teresa Jordan for believing in the relevance of these stories. I also gratefully acknowledge the very capable work of John Alley, who, while not always in full philosophical agreement with these stories, nonetheless recognized the need for them to be told, and Michael Spooner who shepherded this project to fruition.

I owe the greatest debt to Charles "Chas" Peterson and to the Utah Arts Council for providing the network through which a fellow from way down south in Dixie could be heard, and to my wife, Debbie, who trusted through the whole long process that I was writing, and not off daydreaming.

Contents

The originals are nearly gone, and will soon be lost forever in the overwhelming crowd.

Edward Abbey (1927–1989)
Desert Solitaire

Tryin' to make it in this cowboyin' business ain't no easier than ropin' the wind.

Afton Lee (1930–1991)
Somewhere down in Burnt Canyon

U ⊒K U

> *... THE STORY GOES*

something like this:

Down near Mud Spring there's a place called Burnt Canyon. Hellacious spot to lose a cow, Burnt Canyon. You got oak brush thick as molasses. Manzanita tangled so tight a snake couldn't crawl through it. Rest of it's straight up and down. Cow hangs up in there you can just about write 'er off. She's gonna forget she's domestic and return to the wild.

This reporter fella pulls up. He's goin' into Burnt with Afton today. Drives up in his Nissan Pathfinder SE-V6. One of those two-door, four-wheeler, earth wagons stuffed full of backpacks and sandals. Parks that pretty purple outfit next to Afton's multitoned, oft-resurrected '75 Chevy pickup with stock racks.

Reporter fella's got on these African safari pants, come down to about the knee. Apparently he ain't heard about the oak brush in Burnt Canyon. Got on an army surplus overshirt with a T-shirt underneath and a pair of those fancy lace-up hiking boots. Right in style, this fella. Come to get the scoop on us dyin'-breed cowmen. Gonna drop into Burnt lookin' like that.

Afton's had the horses saddled for an hour and a half. Sun's pert' near up. Writer fella walks up with his hand outstretched, "Mr. Lee, I presume?"

"Who'd you think I was, Ulysses S. Grant?" Afton grumbles. "We're runnin' late already."

Formalities out of the way, Afton hands his partner the reins to a tall, sorrel gelding. Then he swings up onto his big bay.

"I hadn't planned on riding," says the reporter. He looks down at the reins as if they're contaminated or something.

Afton spits and pulls his hat down tight. "You're ridin' if you're comin' with me."

Apparently, this reporter fella's been on a horse or two before. He drops the reins and hurries over to his outfit. In two shakes he's changed out of those safari pants into some bleached out jeans that don't say Wrangler or Levi neither one on 'em. He hustles back and throws the reins over the sorrel's neck, adjusts the fanny pack around his waist, and hops three times *before* his foot catches the stirrup. By now, Afton he's fifty yards down the trail.

"Wait for me!" the reporter hollers.

Afton, he's got Burnt Canyon on his mind. He don't hear nothin' else now.

Writer fella comes trottin' up fast, teeth near rattling out of his head. "So what's this horse's name?" he questions.

"Nothin'," Afton replies.

"Surely he has a name."

"Nothin'."

"I can't imagine an animal as fine as this one without a name"

"He's got a name," says Afton.

"And what is it?"

"Nothin'."

"You named your horse Nothing?"

"Did I stutter?"

Next thing you know, the reporter fella is inquiring as to what Afton calls the other horse.

"Nunya Business," Afton replies.

Reporter drops his chin.

"Nunya, for short." . . .

1   Gone to Summer Pasture

1994

THEY GATHERED AT the Upper Well every spring. Twenty or thirty of them returned every year on the same day like swallows with calendars locked in their genetic codes. They pulled up in trucks loaded heavy with horses, saddles cinched to the clattering racks, duffle bags and grub boxes and bedrolls strapped atop the cab. Rumbled right in, they did, and unloaded at headquarters which they called the Upper Well, a name accepted without question for the simple reason that this well was located a couple of miles up the wash from the Lower Well.

The Upper Well sat, and still does, at the bottom of Bull Valley Wash, a channel that runs dry most all the time except for those rare moments following a cloudburst. Bull Valley Wash pushes southeasterly, cutting a crusted gorge through a lonely, gray stretch of southern Nevada and crossing into Utah just before it forks into the much larger Beaver Dam Wash. There at the Upper Well the cowmen who wintered in the Lime Mountain country had rendezvoused for the spring ride for as long as anyone could remember. In the space of a week, those two-dozen cowboys could gather more than a thousand head of mother cows, many of them with slick new calves, from every corner of a vast, Joshua-studded range. From there they trailed most of the herd northward to summer pasture on Clover Mountain.

That was thirty springs ago.

Last spring you could have counted the entire crew at the Upper Well on one hand, and if they gathered two hundred head, they did well.

The old hands are gone now, those leather-faced, chappy-lipped, gravelvoiced old boys, all of them grandsons of Mormon pioneers, all of them living the only life they had ever known—extensions of the lives of their fathers. They harvested a modest livelihood for themselves and their families off the annual and perennial plants and grasses that miraculously sprouted between the rocks and the Joshuas and the meandering dry washes of the Beaver Dam Slope. On soft May evenings they relaxed around the fire on threadbare camp chairs and talked of the cows they had brought in that day and of horses long dead. Men like Max Cannon, Waldo and Frank Simkins, Tal Lytle, Levi Snow, Aaron and Fay and Leo and Glen Leavitt. Horses like Chub and Brandy and Sox and Yeller. They're all gone now—all of them except my father, my uncle, and a few diehards from town who show up whenever they're invited. The rest of them sold out or faded away. Most of them are six feet under, ghost riders in the sky. Their sons lost the dream, or never dreamed it in the first place, and saw no useful reason to carry on. They became carpenters, accountants, and public employees in town. The range is still there, still covered with Indian rice grass, cicardy, June grass, blackbrush, gelleta, bush muly, spiny hopsage, Mormon tea, crested wheat grass, and squirreltail, but the cowboys are gone—most of them, anyway—and so are most of the cows.

1967

Shortly before I became a teenager my father took me to the Upper Well for the first time. We bounced in the cab of a two-ton Chevy cattle truck across the roller-coaster dirt road from Castle Cliff in the deep southwestern corner of Utah, westward to the Beaver Dam Wash. It was a hot, shimmering country, the kind of landscape most would give up for dead. Mile after mile of crusty slopes and sharp draws cut the rolling blanket of desert before us. Endless dry washes wound through it all, gravel-bottomed ribbons that wound down from higher ground, testifying to the fact that it *did* rain once in a while here—very seldom, but very hard when it did. The common term for such dry washes these days is "arroyo," but no one I ever knew called a wash an arroyo. Cattle ranged the entire country; I knew this not because I could see cows, but because my father told me so. You spotted cows on that wide range only on occasion, or if you knew exactly where to look for them.

For me this was a mythical journey, a pilgrimage into the stories I had grown up with. It was my first opportunity to see and touch and live the reality which until now had only been fragments of stories and dreams. The other side of it, which at the time seemed even more monumental, was the fact that I was actually missing school for this. The kids back at East Elementary in my small hometown of St. George, Utah, were, at that very moment, eating their hearts out. I had informed them of where I was going and what I would be doing, and it ranked right up there with the major holidays, maybe even a space launch.

As we dropped into the canyon of the Beaver Dam Wash, I imagined I was in Egypt, the country my less fortunate fellow sixth-graders were studying at the time. A smoothly eroded sandstone cliff on the far side of the gorge looked as if it might have once been the face of the great sphinx. Crossing the shallow, rolling water of the Beaver Dam Wash I felt a twinge of remorse for those kids stuck back there in the hot southeast room of East Elementary, compelled to listen to the low guttural pronouncements of Mr. Sullivan until the clock finally wound around to 3:45. Already, at the age of twelve, I was beginning to bend toward that insatiable longing for freedom which sits at the foundation of every cowboy's constitution.

A couple of miles beyond the Beaver Dam Wash, which is the great gathering gorge of the region's drainage system, we crossed into Nevada and worked our way northward along a rim of the Bull Valley Wash. Our destination was that mythic place I had heard spoken of all my life but had never seen: The Upper Well. The well sat at the foot of a towering, sterile gray monolith called Lime Mountain that jutted out of the landscape like the sharp back of a dinosaur. I soon came to know and to value the fact that Lime Mountain was the most notable brand-name landmark on what to me was an otherwise very generic landscape.

Around midmorning we arrived at a place where the road dropped gently to the bottom of Bull Valley Wash. Dad pointed toward a clump of trees and said that was it. I realized then, as I have many times since, that there are few places on that rocky slope that gained their reputation by what they actually looked like. It is the stories attached to a place which truly make it a place. Without the stories I had associated with it, the Upper Well would have been a profound disappointment.

We pulled into camp, which was bordered on two sides by tall, steep, slate rock ridges. It was a brilliant spring morning, full of sunshine and wind that whipped down the canyon in wild gusts—the kind of wind that will rip the cowboy hat from your head and send it spinning into the brush. More than a dozen cattle trucks were parked among the rocks and creosote—most of them Chevy or GMC cabs with 18-foot beds and red stock racks like my dad's. There were the odd trucks as well: a black International, a light blue Ford, and some pickups of various colors. The trucks added the only element of color to an otherwise bleak scene.

The cowboys had a fire going, not for warmth, of course, but to boil water for coffee and Postum. Though everyone present was aligned in some way with the Church of Jesus Christ of Latter-day Saints, there existed varying degrees of commitment among the men. Several had chosen, at such a distance from the nearest bishop, to forego a few of the rigorous Mormon commandments, most notably Joseph Smith's revealed Word of Wisdom regarding coffee, tobacco, and alcohol. The church-approved pot of Postum sat boiling to the brim in the coals, waiting for the few stalwarts who could face a day on the range without a boost of caffeine.

All the men greeted Dad as he walked up, jabbing him about being late. My father was the youngest of all of them, the new kid on this range. He told them he was late because things don't move as smoothly when you bring the boy along. I trudged up behind him, new straw hat pulled down tight, stiff blue Levis tucked into the tops of boots that weren't broke in yet. I even had on a crisp new western snap shirt Mom had fitted me with especially for the occasion. Dad introduced me as the best help he could come up with, and the cowboys chuckled as they sized me up. I was surprised at how much older they all seemed than my dad. You could see the miles on them; the seasons showed in their wary eyes and in their yellow teeth and in their crooked fingers and in the way they groaned and braced their hips as they stood up. I would soon learn, however, that these apparently slow old fossils were as quick and deft and capable at their jobs as Bart Starr was at his; and that they knew that endless, broken, lonely country better than I knew my way to school. What's more, they rode horses that knew it even better.

I stood next to the fire, very conscious of myself, and watched as they drew their plans in the dirt. I listened hard to what they were saying; their language was foreign to me. The longer they talked, the more my mind and eyes wanted to wander. A few yards away a tall, silver windmill churned fitfully in the breeze. Its blades whistled, then quieted, as the wind built and died. The mill's shaft thunked up and down, hefting water from deep in the gray rocks and spurting it into a huge circular trough made of glittering steel. A giant complex of corrals surrounded the trough, and a few cottonwoods and willow bushes grew around the perimeter. The fences were stockade style—one gray cedar post set against another, tight as a braid, forming a solid barrier against even the most cantankerous cow. Everywhere I looked I saw rocks—the sharp jagged rocks along the ledges above and the rounded, smooth rocks inlaid with swirling pastel patterns across the wash bottoms. Where there weren't rocks, there were creosote or blackbrush or Brigham tea, yucca, oos, or sand—more sand than anything.

Up the bank a short way stood a weathered brown clapboard shack, maybe ten feet by twelve feet. At the time it was called the Upper Well Hilton. In it were a couple of makeshift bunks, and, as my Uncle Eldon always got a kick out of saying, it had "a bathroom as big as all outdoors." Those with seniority slept in the shack. The rest of us slept in the bathroom.

All of this was a bit anticlimactic. The scene and the feelings did not quite link with the dream. But I was there and that was the main thing; and it finally taught me what my father meant by his oft-repeated saying, "The anticipation is always greater than the realization."

Dad didn't waste any time breaking me in. Before daylight the next morning he sent me off to Bracken Pond with Glen Leavitt to gather what cattle might be hanging in that general vicinity. Glen would have been in his early sixties then, an old, old man by my way of thinking. I took the assignment reluctantly, fearing the prospect of having to make conversation with an old man all day. But Glen rode with a sparkle in his eye, and he looked right at me as if he really wanted to know the answers when he asked questions like what grade I was in and if I liked baseball and who my girlfriend was. He wore a dark green work shirt, the kind that looked like part of a handyman's uniform you'd buy at Penney's. Nothing cowboy about his clothing. No hat. And most alarming of all, he wore lace-up leather work shoes. He looked more like a construction worker than a cowboy. Later I learned that he, just as my dad and most of the others, didn't make his entire living punching cows. He had a town job, too.

We weren't even finished with the small talk when Glen all of a sudden decided it was time to split up. I quite liked the idea of team riding, but there's too much country on the slope for cowboys to ride long together. He sent me on a wide circle, alone, off around a distant knoll, to pick up anything roaming out that way. He instructed me to meet him at Bracken Pond, just down the wash from where we split, as soon as I'd finished the circle.

I rode off into the desolate landscape and promptly got lost.

For four or five hours, which in twelve-year-old time is something like forty days, I wandered aimlessly in the wilderness. I was aboard the stalwart sorrel gelding named Judge. Panic had pretty much diluted what little common sense I possessed at the time; it didn't occur to me that my horse might know the country better than I did. My only reference was that razorback ridge called Lime Mountain that stood before me like Mount Sinai. I took Judge in circles, crossing our own tracks a halfdozen times before the muddy little bog called Bracken Pond finally appeared like a miracle. During those terrifying, lonely hours of delirium I began to develop a deep respect for the men who had ridden that country for decades before me.

My hopes would rise, and then they'd tumble. When they hit bottom I saw myself lying lifeless on the rocks, head resting in the prickly branches of a blackbrush clump, flies buzzing across my sun-blistered lips. Before long, tears were trickling down my dusty, freckled cheek at the ultimate thought of crows pecking out my dead eyes. Fortunately, the miracle of the pond's appearance occurred before things grew completely out of hand.

Glen sat like an old prophet on a rock above the thick brown water of Bracken Pond. His horse was tied to a lone juniper twenty feet away. Joy gushed through my heart like a summer flash flood. In the space of a millisecond I was transformed from dead boy in the desert to horseback cowboy headed for camp.

I would later learn that Glen had been back to camp with two herds of cattle that day, many of them cows I should have gathered myself had I not been wandering aimlessly in the desert.

It was late in the day when Glen and I topped the ridge above the Upper Well. We arrived with a dozen more head. At the sight of camp a gust of glory swept my spirit to the sky. There were two hundred head of cattle milling in a cloud of dust in the corrals at canyon bottom. They bellowed and moaned and whined, sending up a harsh and discordant concert. In one day all those cows had been flushed from the draws and flats and far corners of the range, not one of them visible from the road that morning. And now there they stood together inside the solid stockade fence, slowly settling for the evening, waiting for the long northward push that would soon begin.

I spent the next five days eating corned beef sandwiches and Vienna sausages, nursing flaming red saddle sores, popping through blackbrush, listening to cattle bawl, and generally thriving on stories. We got the job done that spring. And we did it again the next year, and the next. But each spring since that first one, there have been a few less cows to gather and a few less cowboys to gather them. This last spring it came down to my Dad, my Uncle Eldon, and a handful of mercenaries who heard about it across the coffee counters at Denny's and Dick's. I was on deadline and couldn't even make it myself. It took them a day and a half to gather and one more to truck the cattle to the mountain.

The old clapboard line shack still stands at the Upper Well. Afton Lee remodeled it a couple of years before he died. The job turned out so well they renamed it the Upper Well Waldorf. Its bathroom is still as spacious and clean and beautifully decorated as it ever was.

ᑌ ∃ᛕ ᑌ

... *"WE'RE GOING WHERE?"*

the reporter fella asks.

"Mud," Afton replies.

"What's Mud?"

"You'll know it when you see it," says Afton. He rides headlong into the canyon, chewing a twig, looking awfully serious.

Long ride into Burnt. Kind of ride you like to share with somebody who can tell a story or appreciate a good one. Reporter fella, he's got no stories. Just questions. Afton's chewing that twig like a beaver.

"William is my name," says the reporter.

"They call you Bill, then," Afton says.

"No, sir. I go by William."

"Well, I'll be . . ," says Afton. He shakes his head and rubs his chin. "I don't imagine there was never nobody called himself William rode down this canyon before."

"So, Mr. Lee . . ."

"Name's Afton."

"Afton," says William. "What relation are you to John D.?"

"Great grandson," responds Afton. "What's it to you?"

"I've always been fascinated by the man," says William. "The way I read things, John D. Lee was one of the foremost figures in the colonization of this region. He played a major role—the massacre notwithstanding."

"Notwithstanding," Afton says, nodding his head to the rhythm of his singlefooting horse.

"He got a bum rap for that Mountain Meadows Massacre," says William. "All of that tended to overshadow his great contributions to history."

"How is it you know so much about my ancestry?" asks Afton. He glances back at William with a suspicious glare in his eyes. He sees William there, chin bobbing, thin hair fluttering in the morning breeze.

"I minored in history," answers William. "I've read everything Juanita Brooks ever wrote. That's where you find the whole story, the full context.

Not just the nutshell stories folks like to hear. When you put it all into context, he comes out an extraordinary man."

"Context," says Afton. He perks up in the saddle and sets his sights on Burnt Canyon. . . .

2   The Heart of the Myth

There was a time and not so very long ago when ranching was a way of life, and a good one.

—Edward Abbey, *Desert Solitaire*

AT THE TIME I didn't know a fresh Edward Abbey essay had just appeared in *Harper's*, a long polemical piece which brutally assassinated the character of anyone who ever swung a leg over a saddle and rode in the dust of a cow. I suppose I should have expected it. I knew nothing was sacred to Edward Abbey, not even cows. But I possessed a monumental weakness where Abbey was concerned: in spite of the fact that I took issue with much of *what* he wrote, I greatly admired the *way* he wrote it. That's why I went to Moab.

Edward Abbey was backlit by midafternoon sun as he stepped into the lobby of Pack Creek Ranch. He was taller than I remembered and not quite so lean. I arose from my seat on the nauga-hide couch and could almost feel him size me up with eyes that wore a permanent, scrutinizing squint. I had met him once before. It had been a quick, small-talk session that began with a limp, halfhearted handshake. This time the interview was pre-arranged and the venerable writer seemed to offer me a bit of benefit-of-the-doubt credibility. His elfin face transfixed into a full smile as he shook my hand, firmly this time. His salt-and-pepper beard was fluffy like a not-too-serious rain cloud, and he had on a short-sleeved western snap shirt, beige Levi's, and plain bull-hide boots with some miles on them.

He came across as very kind and I caught myself wondering if this could be an imposter, if this outwardly cordial fellow could truly be the curmudgeon who brazenly bashed so many of our national icons. The two of us sat down in the lobby chairs—along with our host Ken Sleight and my friend Milo McCowan, the real estate developer and book collector who had arranged the meeting—and began a conversation that lasted for six hours.

Right out of the gate, any lingering question of false identity was left abruptly in the dust. Abbey slipped to the rail and settled in on issues of particular interest to him at the time. He criticized the National Park Service for transforming many of our most popular parks into mini-metro centers. He damned the damnation of Glen Canyon and lauded Larry McMurtry's recent *Lonesome Dove*. He praised another novelist, a fellow from El Paso named Cormac McCarthy whose work he had just discovered (this a full five years before *All The Pretty Horses* and the ensuing Border Trilogy). He also set forth his proposal for legislatively limiting population, suggesting we seal off all our borders to immigrants.

It was inevitable that on the backstretch and final turn, our conversation would ultimately grind down to cattle and the public lands. It was Abbey's race and he held his half-length lead wire to wire. He knew I was the son of a rancher who, like most others in our region, depended to some degree on use of the public range. Still, he held nothing back. He plowed down the homestretch with the same reasoning, the same vitrolic rhetoric, and many of the same patented Abbey phrases that I would read a short time later in his essay. "There's something wrong at the heart of our most popular American myth— the cowboy and his cow," said Abbey. "Some of these cattlemen are nothing more than welfare parasites. They've been getting a free ride on the public lands for over a century, and I think it's time we phased it out. I'm in favor of putting the public lands livestock grazers out of business."

I had figured I was prepared for most anything Abbey might throw. But this one brushed me back. My throat went dry as a desert wind. Obviously I did not agree. I wondered if he was testing me. I knew that Abbey was always one to rile things up—throw a fly in the ointment— just to get your attention. Surely he was joking. But he didn't flinch. He was serious. "We don't need the public lands beef industry," Abbey said. "The vast majority of our beef is grown on private land in the

Midwest and South and East—where you can support a cow on a half-acre rather than the twenty-five to fifty acres it takes to sustain a cow on the public lands of the West." I'd heard his facts before. It was not the facts I disputed so much as the way he strung them together—and the facts that he conveniently avoided.

"Furthermore," Abbey went on, "we'd save money in taxes we now pay for various subsidies to these public lands cattlemen. Subsidies for things like range improvement—tree chaining, sagebrush clearing, mesquite poisoning, disease control, predator trapping, fencing, wells, stock ponds, roads."

It was my turn now. "The last time the Bureau of Land Management cleared any sagebrush for my father, a rancher from Texas was president," I countered. I added that the only range improvements made on his public range allotment in the last ten years had been made largely at his own expense—to the tune of more than $20,000.

But Abbey was on his soapbox now. "Cattle are doing intolerable damage to our public lands," he said. "Almost anywhere you go in the American West you find hordes of these ugly, clumsy, stupid, bawling, stinky, fly-covered, shit-smeared, disease-spreading brutes. They are a pest and a plague."

My chest swelled. No wonder the tables were turning. No wonder the BLM was cutting range rights every year, putting range improvements on hold, and generally making life miserable for folks trying to hold onto their investment and to a way of life on the public lands. No wonder so many ranching families were selling out after four or five generations in the business. I couldn't come up with an eloquent counter to Abbey's diatribe. My defense floated in some vague notion at the heart of the myth he was talking about: that we are choking out one more productive way of life, leaving the land and flocking to the office where the only thing we produce is paper for the recycling bin.

I suppose Abbey was reading my mind. He came back with this: "It's not easy to argue that we should do away with cattle ranching. The cowboy myth gets in the way. But if all of our 31,000 public land ranchers quit tomorrow, we'd never miss them."

"*You* wouldn't," I said. "But I miss a whole bunch of them already. Guys like Waldo Simkins, Aaron Leavitt, Max Cannon, Levi Snow. They're all gone now, and nobody replaced them. Their sons headed into more promising futures; the cows were sold off; their private property was optioned for real estate development; all those generations of ranching, of production, of wealth generated from a renewable natural resource—all of it ended just like that." I could think of a dozen sons of ranchers I graduated from high school with in 1973. None of us stayed in ranching. Not so much because we didn't want to, but because we could see easier and more lucrative ways to make a living. Over the past twenty years, cattle numbers on the public ranges have fallen by the thousands as one ranching operation after another has faded. My father, and others like him, saw it coming for a long time. They sent their sons to college and trade schools—talked them into dentistry, diesel mechanics, financial planning, medieval literature. "There's no future on the ranch," my dad once told me. "If cattle prices or drought don't bury you, the government will."

Abbey railed on and I was stuck there like a trapped coyote. No choice but to listen. He suggested a few methods for reducing cattle on the public ranges—Abbeyisms like declaring a hunting season on range cattle or stocking water holes with alligators. I figured he had said just about every disparaging thing possible. Then he started to get more personal. "Most ranchers don't work very hard," he said. "They have a lot of leisure time for politics and bellyaching. Anytime you go into a small western town you'll find them at the nearest drug, sitting around all morning drinking coffee, talking about their tax breaks."

It was obvious now that Abbey's cowboy and mine were two different breeds. After reading his essay later, I learned that the cowboy image he had fixed upon was cut from the pattern of a no-account, drunken New Mexican he had known back in 1947, who took pot-shots at jackrabbits and road signs with a .44, and let his 40 acres go to tumbleweed. My image came from somewhere else. It was shaped by men like Levi Snow, a slight, gentle, competent man who spent his days eking a living off the desolate range along the Beaver Dam Slope in southwestern Utah and southern Nevada. Abbey's cowboy was exploitive, lazy, and antisocial. Mine was a hard-working man with a set of ethics, some civicmindedness, and a modest fear of God.

I had sense enough to know that most cowboys fall somewhere between the two extremes. I also knew, and was willing to concede, that there have been plenty of cowmen who have made mistakes, who whether through greed or ignorance or even laziness have damaged the land and left behind a sad legacy. But I believed that more of them fit my definition than Abbey's. Of the two dozen true cowboys I had known, all of them built in the mold of Levi Snow, none vaguely resembled the slouch Edward Abbey planted in the minds of a quarter-million *Harper's* readers.

I wanted somehow to share Levi Snow with Edward Abbey. I wanted to tell him that I didn't believe Levi ever sat at the counter of a drugstore. That he wouldn't have had time for politics or bellyaching. That he had cows out on the Slope which he tended like children, hay-fields to mow and rake and bale, fences to mend, calves to wean, ditches to dig, horses to break, strays to gather, ice on ponds to break, grazing fees to pay, taxes to catch up on, rain to pray for, buyers to see, cattle to move, trucks to load, flats to fix, and bills and bills and bills to pay. But I didn't know how to tell him; or maybe I just didn't have the courage.

Yet the image was there, alive and burning on the ridges of my mind. The image of a good and caring man who started every day before the sun, whose quitting time was when everything was done. He had a home and a family in town, but he spent most of his days on the range, camping in a dugout or a line shack or under the stars. He grazed his cattle mostly on the public range, when and how the BLM and Forest Service mandated, and tried his best to make an honest living.

Abbey, I was certain, would have been unaffected by my description. He continued with zeal. "We don't need cowboys or ranchers any-more," he said. "We've carried them on our backs long enough."

I sank into memories. Struggling to protect myself from Abbey's flaying, I recalled a dark rainy spring day nearly twenty years earlier.

Where I come from rain is the greatest gift, the only gift I ever heard my Dad ask for. (I do remember one time when he wished for a million dollars. "What would you do with a million dollars?" I asked. "I'd run cattle until it was all gone," he said.) We were pushing cows up the mountain, up the steep road through Ash Spring toward Bunker Peak. We had two hundred head of bolly-faced cows ahead of us, the best horses in the county beneath us, and a million gallons of water toppling down upon us. Soaked to the bone, we drove those cows up the mucky winding road to summer pasture and the old cowboys hummed and told stories all the way. Levi Snow is the one I remember best from that day. He was short, lean, wouldn't have weighed more than a hundred and a quarter. Kindest eyes I ever saw. Levi was so small some of the other cowboys complained that it wasn't fair; he could weave between the raindrops and not get wet. He wore a tan slicker that covered his frail frame and hung down over his saddle like a dress. His wide-brimmed hat, water trailing off the back, kept his face and ears dry. It was cold and uncomfortable and not an easy thing to be doing. But he was happy.

"We don't need ranchers anymore." The force of Abbey's voice hit me like a two-by-four across the side of the head. "They've had their free ride. It's time they learned to support themselves." When Abbey finally finished, I mustered one last question. He had earlier complained about his modest earnings as a writer, and I wanted to know what he would do if he ever fell into a large sum of money. He thought for a moment, undoubtedly mulling over the paradoxes that underlie his legend. His face, lit by an old wagonwheel lamp, slowly formed a facetious grin and finally he said, "I'd probably buy myself a ranch."

U ⊒K U

*. . . "HOW FAR TO
Mud Spring?"*

"'Bout an hour more," says Afton. "Thirty minutes if not for this heathen oak brush." Afton's face turns sour. The thought of it irks him. "Time was when a man could ride through here in a fraction of what it takes now. 'Course that was in the days when cattle ran in this country."

"But cattle run here now," says William the reporter.

"Nothin' like they used to," replies Afton. "Just a long-ear here and there—like the brindle bull we're goin' after today." His pants hook on a sharp oak branch and he utters a phrase the likes of which even the hardest-nosed reporter seldom hears. "Used to be ten head to every one head now. When there was cattle in this country they kept it open. You had plenty of trails and room to move. Deer, too. The deer can't even negotiate it anymore. Whole cursed place has turned into a jungle. 'Least the cows kept it opened up."

"You're telling me it wasn't always like this?"

"Not by a long shot."

"When did it start closing in?"

"When they started cutting the cattle numbers."

"BLM?"

"Who else?"

"But what about overgrazing?"

"Nobody ever defined that for me."

"Too many cows grazing too little range."

"There was years when this country had too many cows on it," Afton admits. "Especially back in the early part of the century before the Taylor Grazing Act came in."

"That was 1934," says William.

"You're correct," says Afton. "In those days it was every man for himself. A lot of 'em got greedy and overdid it. But once the BLM came in they got it under control, and they've been controllin' the hell out of it ever since. There's allotments where mistakes were made. But cowmen are awful good

about learning from their mistakes. We ain't in the business of running ourselves out of business—which is exactly what we'd be doing if we was trashin' the land the way people like to think we are. We've got range scientists out here all the time helpin' us figure out how to do things better. If there's a better way to do it, we're gonna try it. But most of those folks have got their mind set on cutting or abolishing grazing altogether. And that, my friend, ain't the answer. They've already cut us down to next to nothin'. This grass was meant to be eaten. It does grow back, you know. So what about undergrazing? Here's what you get when you undergraze."

"What do you propose as the answer?" asks William.

"Right now I propose a few well placed matches," says Afton. "Call it a 'Prescribed Burn' if you want to get technical." . . .

3   Rain and Desert Roots

THE WEATHERMAN SAID we were in for some foul weather. He was wrong. It's raining today.

I know there are places where rain is a four-letter word, but here in Utah's Dixie, rain is good weather. Here, rain is hoped for, prayed for, fasted for, and sometimes even danced for. Here on the edge of the great Mojave Desert, rain is the most precious gift. At least in our family it is.

This appreciation for rain must be genetic. I come from a long line of dust-eating, well-drilling, cloud watchers. I was born this way, and as a child I was conditioned to feel happy when skies were gray, because that was when my father was happiest. On those rare occasions when clouds began to gather, Dad began to sing. I never got tired of the songs. "Rain Drops Keep Falling on My Head," was his favorite. I can still hear him singing that song from the movie *Butch Cassidy and the Sundance Kid* as I followed him horseback through the junipers, their pungent evergreen scent wafting from the branches. I can hear the melody muffled through a sheet of rain that drenched us on a summer afternoon below Doc's Pass where we were supposed to find some cows but none appeared. The rain eventually worked its way inside my slicker and started a cold stream down my back, into my shorts, and on through to the saddle. What began as a bright, comfortable morning turned into a miserable, cold afternoon. But Dad kept on singing.

I never got tired of "Rain Drops Keep Falling on My Head," but sometimes I got tired of "Singing in the Rain." Maybe it was because the movie didn't fit. Somehow, Gene Kelly dancing along a rainy city street, gleefully flipping his umbrella, was not the right image there on

Clover Mountain. On the other hand, "Rain Drops Keep Falling on My Head" drew forth images of Paul Newman and Robert Redford riding hard across a mountain flat, leaving the Pinkerton detectives in their wake. Whenever you rode through those Nevada hills you had to wonder if Butch and Sundance might have once crossed that very trail.

Rain always put a smile on my dad's face and brought a tune to his lips. He could never remember more than a few phrases of a song and I suppose that is why he hums so well. When he got to humming real loud, which was usually when the rain came down the hardest, you knew it was a good time to ask him for things you'd been putting off for the right moment. Things like when he was going to get you that .22 rifle, or if you could maybe drive the truck back to the ranch, even though your legs still lacked a foot of reaching the gas pedal.

For my father, the greatest thing about rain was that it made everything wet. It filled the ponds, replenished the wells, settled the dust. It turned the dry bunch grass green, brought on the June grass, the cicardy, the Indian rice grass, and the no-eatum. Rain transformed the dull brown hills into gleaming mounds of green; it turned the drab gray mountains into sparkling blue castles. Best of all was the smell of wet sage and dry earth turned damp. It was a kind of musty incense that filled the air and drew easily into the senses—the smell of "everything's going to be okay after all."

It took four generations to breed such a love of rain into a modern desk jockey like me. I'm sure the same feeling did not exist in my great-great grandfathers, who came west from the verdant hills and lush forests of New England, Switzerland, Denmark, and Mother England herself. Each of them came west out of faith and religious commitment, leaving the green hills and the constant rains behind and taking up land among the stark rocks and dusty brush of southern Utah and southern Nevada. Their likely ambivalence toward rain in the old country must have soon transformed into a longing for the same in this new, bone-dry place. "This country's so drought-stricken," said one of the old-timers, "we've got frogs upwards of seven years old that haven't yet learned to swim."

It was my great-grandfathers, the sons of those original pioneers, who became the cowmen and the cloudwatchers. From the journals I've read of each, all four of my great-grandfathers were fine cattlemen—and lovers of rain.

Jens Nielson crossed the Plains by handcart in the 1850s and nearly lost a foot to frostbite. He later crossed the Colorado Plateau with 250 others who, in the winter of 1880, tumbled through the Hole-in-the-Rock at Glen Canyon and miraculously crossed to the San Juan country. His son, Hans Joseph, spent the rest of his life horseback, trying to stay out of the way of Paiutes and Navajos, and chasing cattle from one end of that San Juan canyon country to the other.

James William Palmer, the other great-grandfather on my mother's side, fled to Mexico in the 1880s to escape the snares of federal marshals who were cracking down on Mormons with more than one wife. There, in the humble village of Pacheco, he owned the finest stallion in the province. Cattlemen throughout the colonies brought their mares to James Palmer's stud.

Over in Nevada, up on Clover Mountain where white men had once tried to settle and were driven away by the Muddy River Paiutes, Lyman Lafayette Woods built a fine two-story home with a balcony. It was made of pine which he cut with a steam-driven saw. The house stood like a painting against the meadows of a mountain valley as if it had been plucked from his old home place in upstate New York and set back down in this far away place. Lyman's son, Lamond Woods, grew up in that Clover Valley home, and it was out in that far off country where he learned to negotiate effectively with both cattle and horses.

Just through the hills, across the state line into Utah, John George Hafen took up land in a fertile narrow valley along a babbling creek known as the Santa Clara. John George had been born at the foot of alpine slopes in Switzerland and he came to his new home in a state of extreme culture shock. He spoke only thick Swiss when he arrived, and the vast, bleak, landscape must have overwhelmed him. His son Johnny took to the land with a natural zeal. He learned cattle and horses and the range, and became a leader among the group of Swiss farmer-ranchers known as the Santa Clara Cattle Company—an organization which still exists today.

These were my forebears. Cloud watchers, all. And that must be why, though the skies are black today, and everything outside is soaked, I feel like singing.

. . . *"ALL THEY WANTED*
to do was rail a few junipers up on the rim," says Afton. "But the way them
tree-huggers come down on 'em, you'da thought they'd requested a nuclear
holocaust."

William sits rigid in the saddle, shifting now and then to take the pres-
sure off the tender spots. "Railing does seem rather counterproductive," he
says.

"My sore butt," Afton counters. "Can't think of nothin' more productive
than to lay down a section of weed trees. I oughta take you up on the
Simkins Chaining. Now that'd open your eyes to reality. Prettiest stretch of
country on this whole mountain. Wide open for miles, and nothin' but
wall-to-wall grass."

William, he's got a problem with this whole idea of railing. "Here we sit
as a nation," William says, "criticizing South American countries for
destroying their forests, and we send our own government out with chains
strung between Cats to topple trees by the thousands."

"It ain't like this country was always choked to death with juniper trees,"
says Afton. "When the first white settlers came in here they was nary a
cedar tree to be found. Fires kept 'em cleared back in those days. Now we
don't get the fires because we put 'em out, and wise folks such as yourself
won't let us rail, and so this plague of cedar trees has got the run of the
place."

"It's not right to destroy trees on a wholesale scale," says William.

"It ain't right not to," replies Afton. "You gotta give up one thing to get
another in this old world. I'm tellin' you, one clump of grass is worth ten of
them deformed cedar trees."

"What's right is what's natural," says William.

"And what's natural is grass. Them cedar trees, they's weeds. They choke
the grass out, shade the ground, and leave it bare. What we're talking here
is what your fancy-pancy friends would call a biological desert."

Ol' Afton, he looks straight on now. He can feel the steam inside. He's
not supposed to get worked up like this. . . .

4   A Cowboy, and a Good One (1932–)

IN A CRACKLING COPY of *Look* magazine, issued in the early 1940s, there is a photograph of my father kneeling at his chair turned backwards to the dinner table. He's not much more than ten years old and his fingers are clasped, prayer style, beneath his chin. The straps of his overalls run under the collar of a crisp white shirt. My grandfather is kneeling at the head of the table, his tie cinched tight, his spectacles in place, his head bowed as he prays upon a table brimming with food. Next to Grandpa is Grandma, kneeling near the cast-iron stove at the corner of the table nearest the kitchen. Eight children surround the table, each in a distinct, impatient praying position.

My father's pose in this magazine picture, shot by a big-city photojournalist by the name of Earl Theisen, is most notable. While all the others' heads are humbly bowed, Dad's is tilted back, his chin pointing toward the ceiling, eyes wide open as if searching for the deity his righteous father is addressing.

The photo was one of several which illustrated a major feature article by Maurine Whipple about the peculiar Mormon lifestyle of southern Utah. The caption reads, "Morning prayer and evening prayer before a meal were rigid Mormon practices in the old days. Now they have been abandoned by all save a few families such as this one."

I have pulled that ancient copy of *Look* from the shelf many times over the years. Its cover is gone, and there is no indication on the remaining pages of what the issue date might have been. But on page 56 there is a story about Whirlaway, the 1942 Kentucky Derby winner, by Jack Guenther, ace United Press sports writer and turf authority. The fact that articles about a legendary race horse and my father's prayerful family would appear in the same issue of a national magazine is to me strangely prophetic. After all, I am certain that in that photo Dad was not looking up in search of deity. He was dreaming of horses.

My grandfather was not by profession a cowboy, which was a source of despair for Dad through most of his childhood. That was because Dad never wanted to be anything but a cowboy. His father was a college professor, what's more, a professor of the humanities and a writer of histories. Dad took small consolation from the fact that Grandpa, in his younger years, had spent enough time on the range with his own father, my great-grandfather John Hafen, to be considered at least a one-time cowboy.

For Grandpa, the lure of literature had been greater than the call of the range. This could possibly be linked to an accident he suffered as a child which left him blind in one eye and reduced his outdoor activity. Maybe that is what turned him inward and opened his mind to books and a love of words. Of course, he still spent much of his boyhood with cows. After all, his father had been known as the leading cowman of his generation. But two of Grandpa's younger brothers, Guy and Max, became the cowboys of the family, and they were the ones who perpetuated the ranch.

Grandpa left for college as soon as the family strings were cut. I can see him now, seated at a wooden desk in the old Brigham Young Academy, twiddling a pencil and pushing the bawling cattle far into the corners of his mind while Shakespeare poured in like fresh, healing water.

It seems to work that way in agricultural families. Many children of ranchers grow up with a mindset against the rigors and risks of cattle production. A kid who is rousted out of bed early every morning with mucky, cold chores to do will often turn his sights toward the desk jobs that come with a college education. Riding through youth in your father's dust will often set you on a trail toward a more refined life.

Yet it works both ways. A case could be made that you're either born with it or you're not. My Grandpa's two youngest brothers, Orval and Max, were twins born in 1903. Orval, like my grandfather, matriculated to the university as naturally as a cow moves on to summer pasture in May. He became a respected attorney and businessman and later served as a leading senator in the state legislature. He was a thin, refined man whose soft, resonant voice could, at a moment's notice, shift into the resounding trumpet of an orator. He was the man who first pushed for a golf course in our town, at a time when the news of golf's virtues had not yet reached our edge of the desert. Orval was a gentleman, a scholar, a patron of the arts, a true Renaissance man—yet he had come from the same womb, on the same day, as Max.

Max came out a cowboy—not by choice, but by birth. He grew up on the back of a horse. He was short and stocky and tough, gruff of voice and husky in the arms and shoulders. While Orval was off at debating competitions, Max was assembling his herd. He continued to assemble that herd until the day he died in 1988.

In the meantime, Uncle Orval was defending criminal cases, making laws, and enjoying leisurely rides on his horse at a rustic getaway cabin in Padre Canyon. During a two-year stretch through the Great Depression, while Orval was busy trying to tug his town into the twentieth century, Max won more than $800 at rodeos.

Max and Orval were close, as brothers, but their careers were as disparate as a cow pasture and a fairway. "Once in a while I'd go see Orval at the law office," Uncle Max once told me. "I admired him because he was the best at what he did. He accomplished more than he ever knew for the good of this region. But I'd get in that office and all I wanted to do was get out of there, get outside. I didn't give a kick for all those books. Orval was the inside and I was the outside."

It was his Uncle Max's lead that Dad followed. In the same way that many sons of ranchers turn completely away from the life they grew up with, Dad turned his back on the scholarly life of his father. He perceived little value in books or poetry. He yearned for the hands-on life, for cows and horses and days outside.

Those dreams may have originated on hot St. George afternoons when, as a youngster, he played boney horses out back of the house in the shaded rows of grape arbors. Boney horses were as close as kids came to toys in those Depression days. They were the white-crusted bones of cattle, the individual vertebrae, leg joints, hoof bones, which, with their prongs resembling legs and a little imagination added, could be magically transformed into miniature animals. Boys collected them by the dozens, visiting the edges of town where dead cattle had been dragged and left to rot in the dry wash bottoms. A cow's skeleton was a valuable find in those days, a mother lode which could enhance a boy's herd substantially. One dead cow could ressurect into a small herd. Through the power of imagination, death became life, refuse became wealth. Those simple bleached white chunks of bone mystically transformed into elaborate ranches in the backyard dirt of a little boy's universe.

I suspect my father had begun, even at that early age, to develop a desire and a sense for accumulating property and managing it toward its highest and best use, of capitalizing on a natural resource that would otherwise go unused. It must have been that notion, coupled with a natural longing for the out-of-doors and an independent life, as well as a special kinship with the land, that drew him and others like him into ranching.

These are certainly not factors unique to children raised in Mormon families, but the structured religious environment in which my father was raised must have contributed in powerful ways to his becoming a cowboy. He grew up in a family where every accessible natural resource was employed to its fullest. Though Grandpa was not a full-time man of the land, production, whether that was the word used or not, was one of his family's chief concerns. Their large city lot on Tabernacle Street was covered from border to border with gardens and orchards, corrals and a barn. There was even an alfalfa patch to feed the milk cows which my father and his brothers milked daily. Morning and night the family prayed for basic necessities—not the least of which was rain to sustain this circle of life they lived in. For a time during the Depression when Dixie College was suffering through a crisis of transition from Mormon Church to state ownership, citizens of the community paid my grandfather's teaching salary in-kind with vegetables, meat, and firewood. In those commodity-based times, such payment was as good as cash anyway. The social, economic, and religious realities of my father's youth taught him that the practical use of the land and its natural resources—*production*—translated into survival.

In high school, Dad became a Future Farmer of America and raised project steers in the backyard barn. In the summer, when he was not irrigating or thinning beets or bucking hay for farmers in the south fields, he got away to the Dutchman's Ranch with his Uncle Guy to gather cows and drive them to new pastures.

During such excursions he began to learn the range, to know its topography, its flora and fauna, its potential—and to love it. He discovered the joy and the freedom it offered. It was probably not so much the romantic notion of becoming a cowboy, that lured him, but rather the discovery of a place were he fit and felt comfortable. Having grown up in such a highly religious and rigidly structured home among twelve brothers and sisters, he must have felt a tremendous transformation as he rode the open range and spent time with men who, though quite religious in their own right, had settled into less orthodox ways of expressing their faith.

In my father's case, as must have been the case for many young Mormons who chose ranching as their vocation, the choice was both an affirmation of the productive society in which they were raised and an escape from the rigorously outlined lifestyle they felt compelled to live the rest of their lives.

In the 1920s and '30s, herds of cattle fresh off the range were trailed down the streets of St. George and corralled in backyard pens. As a young man my father would lie in bed listening to the weanlings bawl across the valley. While his father studied the classics and the scriptures by the light of a coal oil lamp at his rolltop desk in the parlor, my father must have been experiencing visions of campfires on the range.

Most of Dad's classmates grew up preparing for careers in dentistry, truck driving, auto mechanics, business, but Dad never let go of his dreams of the range. He'd have quit school in a flash for a job on a ranch, but his stern father, the professor of the humanities, expected nothing less than a college education for his sons. Dad got a year of junior college in before he was drafted to fight in Korea. He was shipped to Japan, then on to Korea where he arrived just in time to turn around and come home. The Army didn't impress him, nor did any part of the world it showed him. His spirit was tied to the land of his youth, and he felt nothing inviting beyond the mythic relationships between man and horse and livestock and landscape. All the Army did was release him from the responsibility of finishing college. When he returned home from the war, he was his own man, free to make his own decisions. His father would continue extolling the classics in musty classrooms, but Dad would try to stay outside from now on, and every turn he made would steer him that much closer to becoming a cowboy.

He went away to the northwest with friends to log and make some quick money. From there he journeyed east to the copper mines of Montana. But the red rock country pulled him home like a magnet and he returned to school at Dixie for a short time, just long enough to finish a two-year degree and meet and marry my mother.

Mom, the slim, vivacious, pom-pom girl from the other side of the state, had everything Dad was looking for, including a ranching pedigree. Her father was a lifetime cowman and had carried on one of the finest cattle operations in the San Juan country. Whether Dad ever entertained ideas of working into that setup, I don't know. But no ranch was ever handed to him.

His older brothers, Herschel and Eldon, had started in the tire business, and after Dad married, a job at the tire shop was his best option. He and Mom started their family on the hourly wages he brought home from the tire shop. He sweated away the years twisting lug nuts, busting truck tires, patching tubes. Through it all, he never let loose of the dream. He always had a horse, and his idea of recreation was to jump his pony into the back of the pickup and head for Hell's Kitchen down on Lake Mead where there were burros to chase, or up to Hamblin Valley where plenty of mustangs roamed the hills.

On week nights he could be found out at the Posse Grounds, a rodeo arena built and owned by the only civic club my father ever joined.

While other boys' dads went off to Kiwanis or Lions or Rotary, mine went off to his Washington County Sheriff's Posse meetings. Its members, all of them horsemen of some degree, used the group as an easily justifiable excuse to ride on a regular basis. As the wives grew more and more aware of the effect this club could have on their marital status, they formed the Posse-ettes and began to ride with their husbands.

Once in a while, such as one summer in the early 1960s when a troop of Boy Scouts was washed out of the Zion Narrows, the Sheriff's Posse was officially called out to ride. For days, they rode the banks of the Virgin River, mile after mile of it, in a fruitles search for bodies.

During those years Dad's cowboy dreams were put on hold. I remember him coming home some nights tired and aching from the tire shop. He'd shed his rubberblackened clothes, take a hot shower, and lie down on the living room carpet beneath the flickering TV set. Usually he'd go to sleep within minutes, but on nights when he was in an especially good mood he would pop up onto his hands and knees and let me climb on. I'd strap a belt around his chest and hold it with one hand like a bull rider. Dad would begin to buck and spin. I'd hang tight and ride him until he collapsed. Then he'd sprawl spread-eagled on his back and call out in his big rodeo-announcer voice:

"He's a cowboy, and a good one—been to the pay window many times."

I always thought he was saying it about me, but he might have been dreaming it for himself.

Dad could only grasp at his dreams through artificial means, riding in gymkanas and making the occasional weekend mustang chase. He learned to rope during that period and competed in local jackpot ropings and amateur rodeos across the county. Some of his horses were fast, and he wasn't shy about entering them in a local race now and then. Horse racing was a passion that grew and churned in him and might have consumed him if he hadn't finally gotten the ranch.

It happened during that era in the early 1960s when we lost Kennedy and got the Beatles. Dad didn't have any use for either. I know he was moved by the human tragedy of the president's assassination, but he had voted for Nixon, spoken out strongly for Nixon, and he had never seen anything he cared for in Kennedy. He always said that if Kennedy had not died in office, history would have treated him as no more than an average president. It was the same with the Beatles. Dad violently slammed the TV off that Sunday night when they first appeared on the Ed Sullivan Show. He could never see the use in anything so frivolous as four mop-headed smart alecks rattling their heads and spouting such inane lyrics as, "I wanna hold your hand."

In spite of the world-changing events exploding around him in the early 60s, Dad kept his sights sharp. He wanted a ranch. And the way he finally got one was by teaming with his brothers Herschel and Eldon, forming Hafen Bros., Inc., and working out the financing for the old Fred Woods place in Clover Valley, Nevada. Fred was Dad's mother's brother, a fine, traditional cowboy who had held together much of the ranch that his father, Lamond Woods, had assembled. Clover Valley had been my Grandma's girlhood home. She was born there and grew up in a pine-board house just across the valley from the one her Grandfather had built in 1870 when he settled the valley.

From the beginning, none of the brothers held even a remote hope of the ranch providing a livelihood for their families. They would each continue to work and draw a wage from the tire shop for the next twenty-five years. The ranch became their stake in the future and their full-time avocation.

They started out with sixty head and about six hundred acres of private ground in Clover Valley, just right for a base operation. Much of that ground was lush timothy grass meadow that waved gracefully in the summer breeze beneath juniper and pine studded hills. Most of the meadow grass was put up as hay for winter feeding and for horses, which meant that much more grazing ground was needed. The rest of the ranch belonged to the federal government, or more specifically, the Bureau of Land Management. Dad and his brothers bought the permit for summer grazing on Clover Mountain and winter grazing rights twenty miles south on the blackbrush slopes above the Beaver

Dam Wash. A dozen other cowmen owned grazing rights on the same allotments at the time. Names like Simkins, Leavitt, Lytle, Snow, and Cannon, were rooted as deep in that range as the creosote. These were the old cowmen who would become Dad's mentors. They were the men who taught my father the lay of the land and the way cows moved across it.

Dad took to the range like a kid with a new toy. After three seasons he knew the vast country's layout better than most people know their way to work. From the Lower Well, down in the slate-crusted Bull Valley Wash, all the way up to the Ponderosa pines of Bunker Peak, Dad welded the landscape into his senses. He learned that new heifers kicked into the Ash Spring country would likely be found in the fall all the way down in Dodge Wash. He discovered that cows with early calves did best on the Beaver Dam Seedplot. And he found out the hard way that it's hell to lose a cow in Burnt Canyon. When the weaners were sold in the fall, every penny went back on the note. Some years it was barely enough to pay the interest.

On paper it had looked good. He paid under one dollar per animal-unit-month to the BLM for public grazing. But cattle prices were depressed during those years, as they are during all but a couple of years every decade, and when he figured up the cost of supplemental feed, the truck bills, the gas bills, the vet bills, the taxes, the equipment, the interest, and the loan payment, there was never a dime left. A good calf crop, which meant fifty-five calves out of the sixty cows, improved the outlook. But more often than not, the calf crop slipped to below fifty. A bad winter, an outbreak of pinkeye, even one rustler's visit, could turn the outside chance of a small profit into a puff of silly dreams.

Dad was nearly fifty years old before he got out of the tire shop for good. Finally, after more than a quarter-century searching for a way to make his living on the range, he was offered a job running a four hundred-head herd owned by a well-off retired trucking executive. After all those years, the dream had become real. He awoke every morning now with cattle to take care of—no more truck rims, no more flat repairs ever. He had become the foreman of a big operation, and it didn't matter that they weren't his own animals. All that mattered was that now he worked full-time outside. He ran the herd as if it was his own, and finally, life was constantly enjoyable.

Through the years Dad had never been disillusioned. Disappointed, yes, and often. But never disillusioned. One night when I was about twelve years old, Dad walked in the back door of our house covered with mud. His eyes had a sad glaze across them and when Mom greeted him he spoke in a near whisper. I always hurried to the door when Dad got home. It was a habit rooted to my youngest days when the sound of Dad at the back door was the happiest part of the day. That night he wasn't ready to ramble through the small-talk ritual we usually acted out when he got home. He took off his clothes in silence and headed for the bathroom. I knew something was very wrong when I heard him fill the tub. He always showered. After he had time to settle into the hot water, I asked him, through the door, about his muddy clothes.

"The truck got stuck," was all he said.

The next day we got the rest of the story, complete with a Polaroid Instant Camera print. The night before, Dad had been crossing the Beaver Dam Wash in high water just south of Tal Lytle's place. Normally the wash ran no more than a foot or so deep. But rains up in the headwater country had sent some fairly strong waves down, yet not so threatening that Dad didn't think he could cross. He gave it a go just as the sun was falling behind the Slope. Midway through, water swamped the engine and it wouldn't restart. Dad had no choice but to climb out the window and wade to the east bank. He trotted down to Tal Lytle's adobe brick house and rousted the old boy out to help. They tried for an hour to start Tal's tractor but by the time they did, the truck had already sunk to the steering wheel in the shifting sand of the swift water. I don't know how Dad got home that night. He and a crew of Cat skinners went back the next day to dig the truck out and bring it home for rehabilitation.

Things like that upset Dad. Burned him up inside. But the sour feeling never stayed long. He got over things quickly and could start anew with fresh hope. Still, his temper fuse was always short, which is not the best character trait for a man who works with livestock.

There were plenty of times when Dad should have learned his lesson. Like the late evening when he and I were trying to get back to camp after a taxing day of deer hunting. We had ridden out a long way that day and it was getting dark faster than we were getting back. Dad tried to push old Hector—a tall, brawny bay gelding that had carried him faithfully halfway around the world—through a thick stand of oak brush. Hector started into the brush, then stopped. Dad kicked him once, kicked him again, then turned red in the face. "Git up!" Dad hollered. The disgust in his voice echoed through the evening air and rolled all the way down the canyon. When Hector didn't git up, Dad pulled his beautiful .30-06 Remington from the scabbard and held it high in the air by the barrel. He brought the shiny rosewood stock down like a war axe over Hector's rump, generating Mickey Mantle-like bat speed. The finely finished stock split right down the center. Now Dad was really mad.

One afternoon I was helping Dad catch a filly in a small pipe-panel corral. He tossed a loop over the yearling's head and tried to work his way up to her. When she kept backing away, he took a dally around a pipe on one of the fence panels. No sooner had he cinched the bind tight than the filly flipped over backward, which jerked the fence panel onto Dad's leg. The top of the panel caught Dad on the kneecap and bent his knee backward. I nearly passed out as I helplessly watched his leg buckle in the opposite direction, completely jackknifed, as if he were kneeling down with the knee bent the wrong way. He was nearly two years getting over that one, and there is still a hint of a limp, even on good days.

During the summers, Dad spent much of his time keeping gasoline engines running all across Clover Mountain. The engines powered small pumps that looked like miniature oil rigs. But these rigs drew water, not oil, from deep in the earth. In my father's perspective, water is much more valuable than oil anyway. One summer evening I rode with Dad up to the pump at Rock Canyon. I watched him fire up the motor and walk over to the spout where it jutted into a huge round steel trough. It took about three minutes for the water to come. Dad stood there like a kid waiting for Christmas morning. When the first surge of water finally shot out of the pipe and into the trough, Dad's face turned into a giant smile. He quickly grabbed a tin cup hanging on a nearby post and stuck it under the pulsing stream. He handed it to me the and said, "Have some. It's the finest water in the world." I looked at him and realized in that moment that it was simple pleasures like this he lived for. I drank the water and it was cold and very good. I marvelled at how my father could find so much delight in such an elementary thing. Even now I'm sure that the well at Rock Canyon with its world-class water is one of his major sources of joy.

Ironically, it was the pump at that same well which years later wrecked my father's fingers. Somehow, one simmering summer day, Dad managed to get his hand lodged between the counter weights of the pump and the top of the engine. The fingers of his left hand were smashed beyond recognition. He was two hours getting to the hospital and during that time he contemplated removing the sorry remnants himself. But he held out, and the doctor sewed things back together.

Dad admitted his impatience in that one. But it didn't change anything. A few months later another doctor wired Dad's jaw shut after he had stuck a two-by-four behind a cantankerous cow in a chute and she backed through it, slapping the board across Dad's face and pretty much disintegrating his jaw.

Running cattle in common with other ranchers on public land required a high degree of honesty, and Dad established his quickly. Long-eared calves without a mother were prime temptations for lone cowmen on the range. Dad always brought them in and called around. If the owner didn't surface, the animal became a "company" calf and its proceeds were used to repair fences and build holding corrals or for some other common need of the group. Cattle straying onto Dad's range from other allotments were always handled with the same care given his own, and once they were identified, he put word out to the owners to come and get them.

I remember once as Dad and I rode onto a long-eared yearling bull up near the headwaters of the Beaver Dam Wash, I asked him who the calf belonged to. "Nobody," Dad said.

"Can I have him then?" I asked.

"You can if you want. But he doesn't belong to you."

That's how Dad preached. Nothing pious. No long-winded sermons. Just enough to get the point across. The rest was by example. We spent the afternoon trailing the wild critter through the oakbrush, back to the public view of camp where he would no longer be a temptation to anyone.

Over the years Dad has developed a unique connection with the landscape. He runs his cattle and rides his range with a keen awareness of the land. He knows the plants and the animals and is acutely aware of the nuances of weather. He can sense subtle changes in the land from one day to the next, can with one sweep of the eyes discern new growth, a faint strengthening of green, or a slight decline in the foliage. Thirty years on the same land, coming back to it year after year, he knows its capacity, knows what works and doesn't work, knows the land and its caprices the way he knows his wife.

And there is another connection. It is a spiritual connection which is tied to his own investment of years and is linked to the fact that his grandfather and greatgrandfather rode and worked the same land. My father rides the range very much aware of what has gone on there before; he knows the stories attached to each valley, each spring, each trail. The land's history is not lost on him. He tells its story with attention to detail, with an earnest regard for the truth, with the reverence of a caretaker. Part of his hold on the land is tied to his knowledge that it was not given as a gift, but taken, in a sense, from the Indians who inhabited it before—and a knowledge that it was his own great-grandfather who finally, after failures by others, established a manageable relationship with the native inhabitants of that area.

It is the stories that most endear my father to his friends. He never has trouble recruiting help when there's a job to do, because people enjoy being around him and hearing him talk. More than anything else, my father is a man of stories, which ties him to his own father who, in a more formal way, was also a man of stories. Grandpa told his stories in classrooms. Dad tells his around campfires and through the dim light of kerosene lamps in ranch house kitchens. The stories are catalogued in his mind fifty years deep. They are anecdotes of boyhood, snippets of history, tales of the range, and a lot of good old-fashioned off-colored tales.

I always loved to hear my father tell a story. A favorite was the one he would tell about his great-grandfather Woods who established that first peaceful relationship with the Muddy River Band of the Paiute Indians in Clover Valley, Nevada. The story, no doubt, has enhanced itself over the years, and it reflects the bias and the prejudice of the times, but Dad always seemed to tell it more out of some kind of duty than he did out of pride.

"Great Grandpa Woods brought his family here to settle around 1869," Dad would relate. "There'd been some others who tried before, but the Indians had run 'em off and you know it must've took a lotta courage to try again. They say Grandpa Woods was a stern old man, but apparently he was fairly kind and considerate, too. One afternoon when he was returning to the valley with a load of lumber he caught a band of Indians red-handed stealing fourteen head of his horses out of the meadow. He went to another man in the valley who could interpret the Indian language and talked him into helping him. They saddled up directly and took after those thieves. That night they found the Indians camped in a sandy wash and caught 'em by surprise—held 'em at gun point. One of the Indians got real cocky with the interpreter fellow that Grandpa had brought along. The interpreter threatened the Indian with his gun. Grandpa stepped in and stopped him. Apparently the Indians realized Grandpa was speaking in their behalf and they took a liking to him. They turned over the fourteen horses, and promised to bring back the others they'd stolen in a few days.

"Grandpa, he kept four of the younger Indians as security until the others came back with the rest of the horses. He put 'em to work clearing rocks from a field. When the Indians got back with the horses a few days later, Grandpa butchered a calf and they had a mighty fine feast. The older Indians got to feeling guilty and thought the younger ones who had done the horse stealing ought to be punished. They tied the leader of the raiders to a wagon wheel and started to lay it on him with a whip. After the third lash, Grandpa Woods stepped in and grabbed the whip, hollering, 'This is no way to make friends.' After that they never had any more Indian problems in the valley."

Most of Dad's stories are historical in nature, but some of them are stories for stories' sake. As a boy I was sometimes asked to go check the horses while Dad told a story around the campfire. I'd wander down to the horses and kick rocks around for awhile until I heard the boisterous laughter up at the fire. Then I knew I could go back. Some nights the horses had to be checked more than once.

But most of the stories were fit for boys. I'd listen to them in a trance. They were stories of the men who had ridden the same country that stretched out all around us, and to me, those men became mythological figures. Dad's stories gave life to the men and enlivened the landscape we rode. I remember how I longed to become a part of the stories myself, to be remembered with the same reverence and respect as the old cowboys were.

I didn't realize it then, but my father was progressively becoming a part of the stories himself. And I have since come to understand that it is time, and the telling, that make a story. During those hot, tedious days on the range I was reaching back for the long ago stories, not realizing that I was witnessing the birth of new ones. Now I don't have to reach back any further than my own experience. Now the stories are *of* my father, rather than *by* him. Time, and the telling, have made him part of the myth.

. . . *"Uh, Afton? Could*
we stop a moment?"

"What for?"

"My right leg feels as if it might at any moment shrivel up and blow away."

"Spring's right down here a ways. We'll stop when we get there."

Afton rides on. Sun's pounding like a jackhammer now. He wants to get into Burnt before noon or the whole day's shot. He looks back for William. William has disappeared.

Afton mumbles something certifiably unprintable. He pulls Nunya to a stop and quickly steps down, tossing the reins over the horse's head in the same motion. Nunya's worked up a pretty thick sweat by now. Needs a rest anyway. Afton throws the hind cinch, then the front, and pulls the saddle down. Lets it lay right there in the trail where it falls. Nunya hunches and throws a good hard shake, vibrates like some electric toothbrush, hurls cold sweat in every direction.

"Cut you some slack and this is how you treat me," Afton grumbles. He drops the reins and hobbles over to a soft spot in the needles below a pinion pine. From his pocket he pulls a little plastic pharmacy bottle with a typed label taped to it. He pops the lid, shakes out two tablets, and tosses 'em into his mouth.

Then he lays his head back on a rock and falls to sleep.

Ain't but two minutes before a fly crawls up his nostril. Wakes him from his sweet little slumber.

Nunya, that miserable brown gelding, he's gone. Flat disappeared. . . .

5   Summer of '68

EARLY IN THE summer of 1968, I had helped my father move cattle from the winter range to summer pasture on Clover Mountain. I spent the week dreaming about summer rodeos and craving music.

Some nights I'd sneak out to the cattle truck, dial in a good radio station, and listen for an hour in the dark. In the morning, I'd lie in the bunkroom of the ranch house while Dad and Aaron Leavitt fixed breakfast and discussed world affairs in the kitchen. I didn't sleep much those nights, what with the radio hour around midnight and Aaron Leavitt's incessant bronchial coughing. Some nights, old Aaron hacked and wheezed his sixty-year-smoker cough to within a quarter second of his death. You'd lie there in a cold sweat counting the coughs until he'd finally stop to draw breath. Then you'd hold your own breath until he started the next round. But he was always up at five the next morning, sipping coffee, puffing on a Camel, and talking Dad through breakfast.

Near one midnight in early June that year, I sat in the cab of a cattle truck trying desperately to tune in a decent station. For a week I had been deprived of music, which at that point in my life was second only to being deprived of food. The cattle were all on the mountain now, the job nearly finished, and it was time to catch up on the Top 40.

I felt uneasy out there in the dark listening to rock music while some of the region's finest cowboys snoozed just yards away. But one hit after another filled the dark cab and I was mesmerized. The Beatles sang "Hey Jude," and there was "Ruby Tuesday" by the Stones, and Simon and Garfunkle's "Mrs. Robinson."

Then the music stopped. A news bulletin shot across the airwaves like a jagged crack of lightning, jamming the cab of the cattle truck with a stunning revelation. Bobby Kennedy had been shot.

Alone there in the darkness, I wasn't sure how to react. My stomach tied up inside me, but I didn't grow outwardly emotional. Coming from a highly conservative, Nixon-leaning family, I wasn't supposed to care that much about Bobby Kennedy anyway. But I was moved, deeply. I was moved to the point that the music faded far into the background and I started thinking about some things that thirteen-year-old boys don't think about much. Somehow I knew that I was tuned in live to a pivot in history. I knew that something more than Bobby Kennedy had been lost. I recalled the November day five years earlier when I was walking down the hallway of East Elementary after buying my lunch ticket and Mr. Hughes stormed into the hall with the frantic news that President Kennedy had been shot. There had been the same empty feeling that day. And now I sat behind the wheel of a cattle truck in the middle of a summer's night on Clover Mountain, stunned, and struggling to place all this into my own simple context.

Later I slipped back into the ranch house where I lay wide-eyed in bed for hours.

Early the next morning, wrapped in warm quilts, I listened to the cowboys in the kitchen. Dad was telling Aaron how I planned on entering the bronc riding at the Enterprise American Legion rodeo on the 24th of July. "I wonder if he's a little young yet," Dad said.

"Let the kid ride," Aaron growled. "He's gotta grow up like everybody else."

"I suppose so," Dad said.

"Be happy he ain't out smokin' dope and listenin' to that miserable stuff they call music nowadays," Aaron muttered. "It's a good thing we're still raisin' up a few cowboys. They're the only hope for this here pissaroo of a world."

I lay staring at the cracks on the hundred-year-old ceiling of the ranch house, feeling guilty about my fondness for rock music and thinking that I had let down the Aaron Leavitts of the world. There had to be a way, I figured, to save this pissaroo of a world without abandoning rock 'n roll.

The smell of coffee and the sizzle of bacon and eggs floated into the bunk room. I knew they hadn't heard the night's news. I lay in bed and listened to their chatter, realizing how trivial it would all sound to them if they knew of last night's events in Los Angeles. Aaron Leavitt rambled on in his low growl of a voice. He was of that special breed of cowboy who could save the world over breakfast. He was the one who had taught me never to ride blindly in my father's tracks, but to swing out wide and take my own course so I'd always know where I was and where I'd been. "You stay on your old man's tail and daydream and you'll never know how to get back," he told me. "The only way you learn the country is to make your own trail and see it all pass by."

Aaron's voice was disarming and he always talked as if he had a burr under his blanket. Listening to him talk to Dad that morning was as entertaining as anything I could imagine. "It's time we kicked all those dough-brains outta Washington," he mumbled. "Ain't a one of 'em worth a pinch of sour owl shit. Git some common folks in there. Common sense. That's the only thing that's gonna save this here pissaroo of a world."

I lay motionless in bed a few more minutes, struggling to sort out a confusion of mythic proportions. Finally I got up, pulled on my stiff Wranglers, and went into the kitchen to tell them. . . .

U ⊒K U

. . . "WORTHLESS-NO-ACCOUNT-cross-eyed-splay-footed-somebitch," remarks Afton at the absence of his horse.

Sure enough, tracks head straight down the trail, directly toward Mud Spring where the water is thick, but still plenty wet.

Afton grabs a limb on the pine above him and hoists himself up. He too has been looking forward to a drink. But he's been willing to wait until they could both arrive together. He starts a string of obscenities that stretch all the way to Mud Spring. Some of 'em words he learnt in Sunday school, but used here out of context. He grabs the saddle pad in one hand, the saddle with two ropes tied to it in the other, and tromps down the trail.

One hour later, sweat soaked all the way through his crusty Wranglers, he rounds the bend and lays eyes on Mud Spring. More specifically, lays eyes on Nunya, who's standing in mud up to his belly. Legs stuck like four posts in cement.

Afton reverts back to those Sunday school words, with a few variations to fit the situation. He drops the saddle and pad in the oak brush and sits down on an outcrop of rock to contemplate the circumstances.

About then ol' William trots around the bend, ploppin' in the saddle like a kid who's just dropped two-bits in the slot to ride the plastic pony at K-Mart.

"Here I am!" announces William, "Rested and ready to ride. Say, don't tell me. I'll bet that's Mud Spring!" . . .

6   In Search of the Devil

1969

LANCE HUNTING WAS the consummate cowboy. He was the only student known to have worn a cowboy hat in the halls of Woodward Junior High since the 1940s. Never straying, Lance wore only blue denim Wrangler Cowboy Cuts, Tony Lama bullhide boots, western snap shirts, and a handsome silver-belly Resistol which sat strategically on his jet black head of hair. His religion consisted of the combined words of Charlie Pride, Merle Haggard, and Johnny Cash. He knew all their lyrics and worshipped their souls.

I got to know Lance during a spring cattle drive in the late '60s. He was a tall, gangly, dark-featured kid whose family had just moved to St. George and whose father worked for the D. I. Ranch out at Motaqua on the Beaver Dam Wash. We had classes together at Woodward, and when Lance got wind our outfit would be moving cows for a couple of weeks after school let out, he made himself available.

Under the shadow of Lime Mountain, between the Upper and Lower Wells on the west side of the Beaver Dam Wash, Lance and I developed a close friendship. Together, over the course of two or three days, we assembled a couple hundred cows and calves and dreamed our cowboy dreams.

On a blustery summer morning we started the herd up a dirt road through Cedar Wash, north toward Ash Spring in the direction of summer pasture on Clover Mountain. Lance and I took the herd ourselves that gray morning. It looked an awfully lot like it might rain.

The cattle moved at a limber clip, invigorated by the cool moist air. We rode nonchalantly behind them, swinging out now and then to pull in an errant cow. A tiny rust red calf, maybe a month old, held his tail high and pranced gingerly alongside his mom near the rear of the herd. Every few minutes the calf darted out through the blackbrush like a willowy deer, then charged back into the group. Each time he left he'd venture a little farther out, as if testing us.

"I'm gonna win the world someday," Lance said matter-of-factly as we ambled down the road. His words tumbled out of the sky and rolled softly over me like distant thunder.

I looked at him a little puzzled. He rode on in the hazy morning, his chin bobbing to the rhythm of his horse, and looked straight ahead with conviction. "You dang right," he said, not even turning toward me. Then he pitched his right arm forward, holding the bridle reins of his bay horse high above the dark mane. He threw his legs over the break of the horse's shoulders, feet still in the stirrups. "The summer I graduate—I'm headed down the road."

I knew Lance was serious. Sometimes you weren't sure, but he could talk about serious things in a mature way, like he was twenty-one instead of fourteen. The way he sounded, I couldn't help but believe him. I figured he really *would* go down the road someday.

"You gotta want it," Lance said. His black eyes pierced me now. We trotted down the road to catch up with the cattle, and I silently wished for some kind of conviction as solid as his.

"Bronc ridin'," Lance said as we settled back in behind the herd. "Saddle broncs, the classic event of rodeo. I intend to be a champion." He swung his legs, fore and aft, from the shoulders of his gentle horse to the cantle of the stock saddle. No question he had the talent.

"I hope to have my own ranch some day," I said, but not with the same conviction. The little calf darted into the brush again. "I don't know, maybe I'll be a vet. 'Course, I don't like the thought of spending half my life in school. How you supposed to know what you want?"

"For me there's only one thing," Lance said. "I'm hittin' the circuit."

We weren't two miles out of camp when that springy red calf squirted out of the herd again and cut into the junipers. When he failed to return, Lance whipped his tall bay with the bridle reins and shot out after him. He galloped into the thick trees and soon disappeared. I kept my post at the flank of the herd and caught a quick glimpse of horse and rider between the junipers. Then a sudden flash of red calf. But they were gone again just as quick, gone in a thick forest of waxy green limbs. It was quiet now except for the soft concussion of a few hundred split hooves on the powdery road.

Several minutes later Lance returned calfless.

"Where is he?" I asked.

Lance gave me a blank look. "The little devil's gone—flat disappeared."

"What kind of cowboy are you?"

"He's a devil," Lance said. "I hereby name that disrespectful critter: 'Calf Devil.'"

"I don't care what you call him," I replied. "We gotta find the little sucker."

It wasn't long before the wiry red calf rejoined the herd, sneaking in from the trees.

"You little calf devil," Lance scolded. "We oughta relieve you of your gonads, right here and now."

When Calf Devil left the herd again, I impatiently set out after him. My horse, Old Judge, carried me in hot pursuit, and the faster we wove through the trees and the brush and the cactus, the harder Calf Devil ran. I remembered all the times my dad had hollered at me about swinging wide around calves. "You've got to give them twice as much room as you do a cow," he always instructed. "Otherwise you booger 'em out of their little minds."

Lance deserted the herd and joined the chase, swinging extra wide to help me overtake Calf Devil. I untied my rope, shook loose a loop, and in the process lost sight of the calf.

He was gone.

Lance met me on a small knoll above Cedar Wash, and we wondered aloud to each other what might have become of Calf Devil. We had no choice but to return to the herd and resume the northward push.

"He's gone," Lance said. "I can feel it." He yipped the herd on its way. "Gone forever."

"He'll be back," I said.

"No sir," Lance said, his chin hanging. "I'm afraid we've seen the last of Calf Devil."

Up along the ledges of Ash Spring, several miles from where we'd last seen the red calf, we still wondered about the little beast. Eventually, though, we fell into other topics of discussion.

I told Lance that my great grandfather Lamond Woods had been one of the finest bronc riders in these parts. Lance smiled and said that was how he wished to be remembered. I told him I wasn't sure how I wanted to be remembered.

"Rodeo," Lance sighed as he leaned back in his saddle. "That's all there really is."

"Maybe I could go with you."

"Where the hell's that Calf Devil?"

The next fall Lance's family moved back to Beryl, up on the Escalante Desert. I didn't see him so much after that, except at the rodeos.

1974

YEARS LATER, WHEN Lance was enrolled at Trade Tech and I rodeoed for Dixie College, we sat together in the spectator stands at an intercollegiate rodeo in Ogden. Lance was learning the welding trade and I was still trying to figure out what major to declare. We were watching the last section of bull riding and neither one of us was up.

"Did your dad ever find that little devil of a calf we lost?" Lance asked.

"Not that I know of," I said.

"Calf Devil," Lance sighed. "I still wonder sometimes."

We watched as one bull after another blasted out of the chute, launching cowboys like rockets. I hadn't thought about Calf Devil for a long time. As we sat there, I wondered about him all over again, and thought of the cowboy dreams Lance and I had dreamed out loud as we pushed cattle up the country.

Moments later a chute gate opened. A tall wiry red bull ignited. He shot into the arena as if his legs had thrusters strapped to them, blowing higher with every jump. I'd never seen a bull go so high. The rider made about four seconds before he was ejected into the northern Utah air. Free of the pesky cowboy on his back, the bull ran full speed toward the spectator stands and brushed the fence near where we sat. I caught sight of the brand on the bull's left ribs and nearly fell off the bench. "You're not gonna believe this," I told Lance. "No way are you gonna believe this. That bull's got my dad's brand on him."

Lance stood up and started to get emotional. "That's him!" he yelled. He plowed through two rows of spectators and chased the bull down the fence line in front of the stands. "Stop, you little Calf Devil! Stop!"

U ∃K U

*. . . Nothin' more discouraging
than a horse in the mud. 'Specially if it's the horse that's supposed to carry
you home.*

"What a predicament," says William. He swings out of the saddle and
ties Nothin' to a clump of oak brush. Afton's already removed the thirty-foot
rope from his saddle and he's building himself a little loop.

"What's your plan?" questions William.

"I got no plan," says Afton. "I'm wingin' this one. If I did what part of
me thinks I oughta do, I'd club him over the head with a cedar post and put
us both out of our misery. 'Course then the animal rights folks would crucify
me, plus I'd have to walk back out of this canyon. So I'll do what the other
part of me thinks I oughta do and try to fish the dimwit outa there."

"Is it quicksand?" William wonders.

"Not hardly," says Afton. "Suppose it's the closest thing we got to quicksand in this desert. Enough to make life miserable, anyways."

"Looks hopeless to me," says William.

Afton, he hobbles on around the mud hole and commences to swing his
loop. He lays it nicely over Nunya's head and jerks the slack. To this, Nunya
offers a pitiful whinny.

"Shut up, ya no-account glue-factory candidate," Afton mutters. "Now
cooperate or you'll be standin' in that very spot plumb through eternity."

He commences to tug on the rope, to which Nunya sighs and turns his
head.

"Outa there. Now!"

Nunya doesn't budge.

Afton starts to holler. He fills the canyon with the cloudiest outburst of
expletives you ever heard. He yanks and yells, yanks and yells, until Nunya
lunges forward and sends his master sprawling aback. Afton rolls into the
stiff branches of a manzanita bush. Nunya hops out of the mud and wan-
ders up to him. Afton's stuck in the bush and there stands Nunya, looking
down concerned as can be, dripping that mud all over him.

This is when William makes his big mistake. This is when William
starts to laugh. . . .

7   Twin Canyon

Big bulls in the springtime follered gentle cattle in,
Had come up from the badlands; they was born down there in Twin.

—Melvin Whipple
"It's Been a Long Time, Pardner"

I USED TO stand at the giant picture window in our living room and look southward. Somewhere out beyond the last house, the last barn, the last field, I knew Utah ended and Arizona began. It was a magical thought. I believed I was a privileged kid, living there on the border like that, at the edge of what all the men I knew called the Arizona Strip.

I'd never set foot there. But I knew it was a big country. It was a mythic place, a land unto itself so steeped in lore that you didn't say, "down at the Arizona Strip," or "over in the Arizona Strip." You said, quite respectfully, "Out *on* the Strip."

Standing there at the window, I knew that if I started walking straight south I'd eventually arrive at the most enormous canyon in the world, and at the bottom of that canyon I knew there rolled a mighty river. This I knew only from maps.

It's been a long time, pardner, since we rode that mountain range
Where the tall pine trees grow skyward on that rocky rough terrain,
Where the cedars grow in clusters there among the malapies,
The oak and manzanita and the purple sagebrush thrives.

In the winter of my fourteenth year I finally got onto the Arizona Strip. On the same occasion I witnessed certain cowboy skills for the first and last time. This was just before the old Mathis place at Parashaunt changed hands and became property of the Gubler-Frei outfit. The

Mathises had owned the ranch since the early part of the century, but Reed, the last of the Mathis cowboys, was ready to retire. He'd keep the old place at Pine, not far from the foot of Mt. Dellenbaugh, but the rest of the ranch would become the property of the Gublers and Freis of Santa Clara, who took over in 1970 and ran the place until the people of the United States bought it back in 1985.

Before the Santa Clara cattlemen could take possession, some house cleaning had to be done. Reed Mathis assembled a bunch of free-lance cowpokes for a mission into Twin Canyon, on the upper fringes of the Grand Canyon, to search out and retrieve what few wild and unmarked cattle remained in the pockets, coves, draws, and thickets of one of our planet's roughest sections.

It was an adventure I might just as easily have missed. When Dad shook my shoulder that morning at four o'clock I rolled over and ignored him, coveting sleep more than raw adventure. A minute later Dad called again and said it was my last chance. "Get up or stay home," he said. I dozed again, struggling for another moment's sleep, until the slam of the back door doubled me out of bed. In a quarter second I was in my pants and dragging my boots, shirt, hat, and coat through the house, out the door, and into the departing cattle truck.

When the spring rains brought the flowers, and the early mornin' chill
Made a man glad to be livin' in those Arizona hills.
I am shore that you remember, and would like to be again,
Back a-workin' cattle on that rocky mountain range.

We drove out to the corrals on the northwest edge of town and loaded the horses. Our gear and grub were already strapped to a rack above the cab. We all met at Denny's for breakfast. There was Dad, Clive Burgess, his son Joe, Uncles Herschel and Eldon, cousin Brent, Marv Jones, and Uncle Phil Squire, who came along to record the entire experience on Super 8 movie film. The others—Reed Mathis, Buster Esplin, Earl Sorenson, Bruce Harris, and Uncle Ferrel—would meet us at Slim Waring's place on the Strip.

Belly full of pancakes, sausage, and milk, I took my place alongside Dad in the cab of the truck. We rode into the thick dark morning, out the bottom end of town and onto the fabled Strip. I was wishing I had a friend or two along to share the adventure. I had grown up on stories about the likes of Preston Nutter, Billie Brink, Bill Shanley, and other legendary characters of the Arizona Strip. Dad had told me the story of Wayne Gardner many times—how he froze to death under a tree one winter in the late 40s. He had left his comfortable home in St. George and set out in a storm to check on his sheepherder out in the Pigeon country. His vehicle had broken down and he'd tried to hike in and while he rested beneath a tree, his spirit departed. And there were others. Billie Brink had drowned while swimming his horse across the Colorado River as he brought a herd of cattle onto the Strip from the south. A dozen more stories rattled around in my mind like rocks in a hubcap.

I knew about the modern cattle operations of a handful of families who lived in St. George and still ranched on the Strip. The Atkins, the Blakes, the Bundys, the Esplins, and the Iversons. The Crosbys, the Seegmillers, and the Foremasters. There were other names long rooted in that land as well: Childers, Cox, Heaton, Whipple, Brinkerhoff, Nielson, Leavitt, Shelley, Alldredge, Black, Bowler, Burgess, Schmutz, Snow, Snyder, Sullivan, Spendlove, Waring, Welch, Johnson, Langston, Lauritzen, Reeve, Russell, Andrus, Craig, Carrol, Jensen, Gardner, Gates, Hale, Lytle, Pymm, Sorenson, and Woodbury. Dad had always said that those folks out on the Strip spent their whole lives trying to make enough so they could move to town and buy a nice car. Now everyone wanted to leave town and move back out there.

But as much as they might have wanted to, no one was moving back. The Arizona Strip is one of the most remote regions on earth. It is five million acres of no electricity, no phone lines, and very little water. The lack of water is what kept it remote, plus the reality that the Grand Canyon defines its southern border. The fact that there are 280 miles of canyon with no highway bridge means there's little reason for anyone to pass that way except out of curiosity. And even then it requires a stout vehicle and an even stouter heart.

Somehow that morning I knew I was barely squeezing in on the tail end of an era.

There's trees that's trimmed up, pardner, in quite a lotta draws.
We are the boys that trimmed 'em with a short dehornin' saw.
We've tied wild cattle to 'em, the kind that wouldn't turn er bend,
Wilder than a mule deer, had to rope and lead 'em in.

We drove straight to Mokiak, not stopping at the Slim Waring place at Wildcat where Buster Esplin headquartered and where we'd spend our nights. At Mokiak it was still dark. This was high country—the Shivwits Plateau—and a cold wind rushed through the pines as we climbed out of the heated truck. The wind was boisterous in the ponderosas, so loud it made the morning seem colder than it really was. We unloaded the horses and saddled them in the gray dawn. Marv Jones was excited about the day's prospects and he laughed his high-pitched laugh which ricocheted like a bullet through the trees until it finally escaped into silence. I thought of my friends back in town, how they would just be climbing out of bed with nothing better to look forward to than a spelling test at school. And me? I'd be pushing off through the trees in a matter of minutes, crossing into Lake Mead National Recreation Area, riding into glory, all this while they answered roll in homeroom.

We rode single file through the pines to a clearing. Reed Mathis, the patriarch and leader of our expedition, swung off his horse, and squatted to the ground with the reins in his hand. He cleared away a layer of moist pine needles and began to draw the day's plan in the dirt. We all got off and circled his little makeshift blackboard. It was light enough now to see the lines in Reed's face. He was a handsome man. His hat sat at a dignified angle on his head, and his benign eyes were intent on the world he was drawing there in the earth. He spoke softly as he etched the plan. We all listened hard. We would split into two groups, he said. Each group would ride down a fork of Twin Canyon.

> Those trees are scarred, ol' pardner, where a big steer has been tied,
> And you know before you caught him you shore took one helluva ride.
> Ol' boy, we rode good horses, the best in the trees and rocks,
> They'd shore go straight way to 'em and pack you to yer stock.

"There could be cattle down either draw," Reed said. "Bring anything you find down the canyon, and we'll meet at the fork. Then, depending on our luck, maybe we'll have a little rodeo."

Reed Mathis must have been in his sixties then. He was a small, wiry man, built in the same compact style as most of the best cowboys I knew. I would soon learn that what he lacked in size he more than made up for in savvy, for the man knew his way around a cow.

Now the sun lifted its arching back over the buttes and ledges of the Colorado Plateau and light began to bounce among the sharp rocks. I wished all the guys from school were there. Old Judge carried me true down the steep, narrow trail. In places it barely clung to the canyon's edge, and you could peer off into what seemed to be eternity. Judge's shawed hooves chinked against the broken limestone, filling the cold air with tinkling music. Up ahead, Uncle Eldon turned in his saddle and exclaimed that we looked like the Wild Bunch. That was the year of Newman and Redford's *Butch Cassidy and the Sundance Kid*, and I meandered in thoughts of remorse at having been born a hundred years too late.

Marv Jones rode jovially behind me. He was a connoisseur of such expeditions and would choose something like this over any of the world's finest luxury cruises. I knew what Marv was going to say, so I asked him before he could ask me: "Is the anticipation greater than the realization?"

"Yes," Marv answered in his thundering voice. "But I guaran-damn-tee you, the anticipation ain't worth squat 'less it's followed by some realization."

"Let's go for the realization," I said.

Big bulls in the springtime follered gentle cattle in,
Had come up from the badlands; they was born down there in Twin.
Their horns was long and shiny; they held their heads up high,
Had just come from the bushes, and the sunlight hurt their eyes.

By midmorning we had safely reached the bottom of one fork of Twin Canyon. It was still cold and all the horses were throwing off steam. We loosened the cinches, tied the horses to the closest bush or tree, and lay down under a huge juniper for a nap. But I couldn't sleep. I would have given my hundred dollar savings account for five more minutes in the sack earlier that morning, yet now I couldn't even doze. While the others stretched out on the cold ground, I started wandering. I walked out to a huge rock that hung over an embankment above the dry Twin Canyon Wash and looked up the gorge we'd just come down. We were directly in the vortex of the V, smack in the confluence of two nearly identical canyons. Now I could see up the other canyon, and as I studied the view, I caught sight of a faint cloud of dust. I wondered if it was the other group, or maybe just a little dust storm. I figured it could have even been a rock slide. I had seen a rock slide once in the Grand Canyon on a Boy Scout river trip. It amazed me how we could carry on our trivial human activities beneath all those precariously placed rocks without more of us getting smashed.

But the dust was no rock slide. It was cattle, and their cloud moved steadily closer until the detail of cowboys gallantly in pursuit came clearly into view.

They had never seen a human, so they never wore a brand;
They was just plain damned mavericks that once roamed that brushy
  land.
You kin bet, old pard, we caught 'em and led 'em to a corral,
There was times we had our troubles and quite a lotta hell.

Searching my mind for the best phrase, I came up with, "We've got livestock!" I yelled it as hard as my nervously puffed lungs would allow me to. The cowboys at rest under the tree flew out of their slumber and mounted their horses with the same type of haste I had demonstrated in my bedroom that morning. Cinches tight, ropes in hand, we awaited the clamoring herd.

Uncle Phil rode onto a knoll and pulled his Bell and Howell Super 8 from the saddle bags. From there he captured the entire event for posterity. Twelve head of white-faced cattle wheeled out of the side canyon and into our open area. They were long-eared, wild Herefords, the worst kind. Dad had often told me that a truly wild Hereford will make a snotty Brahma look like Daffy Duck. I knew, as Reed had earlier informed us, that these animals were witnessing the human species for the first time. And it was also quite evident that they were not impressed.

Old Judge shivered beneath me. He knew better than I what was up. My heart pumped in my throat. The adrenaline was starting to brew somewhere inside me and soon it would erupt through my cells like an exploding volcano. Now, as the cattle broke out of the side canyon and into the main channel, they spread like gun-shy deer. I watched Clive Burgess slip directly in and rope a cow. He ducked his horse around a well-anchored juniper and let the cow wrap herself to it. Uncle Eldon shot in after a three-year-old bull, caught him, and Reed Mathis helped him tie the wild-eyed critter to a tree.

"Start a fire," Reed said matter-of-factly.

A cowboy laughed at troubles, we always made a hand,
Yes, it's been a long time, cowboy, since we burnt the Vee Tee brand.
We have popped a lotta bushes, and we've rolled a many a rock.
Buildin to some snaky critter, when they shook a nasty hock.

My cousin Brent and I got off and started a fire with driftwood out of the wash bed. Reed untied a couple of iron rings from his saddle straps. I asked Brent what they were and he couldn't say. Uncle Eldon, Brent's father, looked at us with a twinkle and said, "Guess you boys are a little young for this. Those are runnin' irons. That's what you brand with on the open range."

"Oh."

Within minutes the rings glowed red in the coals. Reed picked up two short sticks and forked them through one of the rings. He squeezed the two sticks together to form a bind on the ring. The bull's legs were tied tight, and Reed walked around the animal like a billiard player sizing up the table. He moved quickly, with smooth, calculated efficiency. You could see the patience in his eyes, yet he wasted no time. His strokes were graceful as he burned the VT into the bull's hide. It was so routine he almost looked bored. I wondered how many head he had branded in a half-century on the Strip. They said in his early days Reed had known Bill Shanley and had ridden with Sam Radliff. It was Radliff who taught him to rope.

I watched the entire proceeding with the awe of a kid at his first major league baseball game. Reed finished and began to untie the bull. "Watch it," he said as the tie rope flew loose. Uncle Eldon was standing too close and the bull kicked him over a bush, and he rolled down an embankment. He completely disappeared and we wondered if he was hurt, but took comfort when his head popped over the horizon and he was laughing.

Reed had let the bull go knowing we would never get him out of the canyon short of quartering him and hanging him over the saddles. At least he was branded, and if he ever did show up on the plateau and by some miracle was corralled, his owner could lay claim to him. But it is likely that he never left the canyon, and remotely possible that some cow might have made it back down into that hole and that the bull could still have progeny in the canyon today.

> Those trees were decorated with the cattle that we tied,
> And the air was shore a-smokin' from the smell of burnin' hide.
> Yer ol' hoss is excited, and the blood pounds in yer brain,
> When yer bustin' through the cedars pullin' on those bridle reins.

We tied Clive's cow to a solid tree with a halter knot so she wouldn't choke. We'd take her out later with the rest of the driveable cattle we could gather. Meantime, Dad, Buster, Earl, Bruce, and others had caught livestock and either branded them or just tied them up awaiting further instruction. By midafternoon we had assembled a sizeable herd, and we began to push them up the canyon toward camp.

Earl Sorenson's muscular bay gelding moved up the trail slowly, as if each step might be his last. Close inspection revealed what seemed to be a broken blood vessel in a hind leg, and there was a nasty gash on the horse's brisket, most likely a puncture from one of the many long-horns we'd encountered. The bay was exhausted and walked only a step or two at a time now. He kept stopping to blow and it looked awfully hopeless.

Brent offered to lead the horse out, so Earl got on Brent's horse and Brent and I took turns leading the ailing gelding afoot and riding Judge. The others rode out ahead of us with the cattle, leaving Brent and me alone in the canyon with one good horse and an almost dead one. They'd pick us up on the road at the top.

It took hours to get the horse out of the canyon. Darkness fell before we topped out. We were cold and hungry. We tried to humor each other by talking about the state basketball finals coming up and Dixie High's chances for a fine showing. On the surface we smiled and chuckled, but inside we were both terrified. When we finally got to the road we tied the sick horse to a pine tree and stood waiting in the cold night air.

"One of those Prince Burgers from the Frost Top with bacon and tomatoes and French fries with tartar sauce would sure taste good right now," Brent said. I could have cuffed him for saying it, but we were cousins and good friends. I just laughed and let it ride. Soon we started naming everything that was good: pronto pups, chocolate-marshmal-low shakes, strawberry shortcake. My stomach churned and my mouth drooled. It had been a long time since breakfast.

We each took a sweaty saddle blanket and spread them under a tree. Lying on my back and peering up through the thick pine branches, I could see stars emerging now. The world seemed infinitely huge. Home was as far away as Alpha Centari and I grew colder watching

Earl's horse quiver with every breath. Starlight glistened over the sweaty glaze that coated the gelding. It must have been a deep and painful fever.

Brent finally got up and walked down the road a stretch, seriously hoping to encounter the others. I was alone now in the night and stories began to stream through my head like slow moving trains.

The Arizona Strip was no longer a mythic geography in my mind, but real and palpable; I was lying on the Strip, under the stars, no longer just a hearer of the stories, but actually becoming a part of one myself. In spite of the hunger and terror that gripped me, I clung to the moment as if it were a precious nugget I'd been panning for forever. Along about midnight, eighteen hours since breakfast, I heard the sweet sound of the truck.

We've made a lot of horse tracks, seen a many long ol' day,
The smoke from brandin' fires scattered all along the way.

Dad backed the truck up to an embankment near the road. The golden stream of the headlights arced and swung through the trees. We loaded Judge and the sick and injured horse in the truck. When I climbed into the cab, Dad handed me an apple. It was a simple act, but one I've always remembered. The cab was lit only by the weak glow of the dash. As he reached the apple toward me I felt the respect in his eyes. He knew how hungry I was and he knew this had been a day of initiation for me. In that frozen moment, our father–son relationship moved a notch closer to man-to-man. And no apple ever tasted so good.

We drove back to Wildcat, which is the old Slim Waring place that Buster Esplin has run since the 1950s. Supper was still a half hour off so I took a seat on the couch, crunched between two sweaty cowboys, and listened to stories of the Arizona Strip. Uncle Ferrel related the entire Jack Weston affair, as he remembered it. Jack Weston had died of a sheriff's gunshot wound not far from where we sat. His accomplice wife had buried him in a shallow grave from which the authorities dug him up for identification once they caught them. I had seen a picture of the grisly scene and now that image overpowered my thoughts—until the subject changed back to the day's events.

Reed, who sat comfortably in a rocking chair, kidded Bruce Harris about losing his hat earlier in the day. A gust of wind had whipped the new hat, bought especially for this occasion, off Bruce's head. The hat tumbled over the edge of the canyon and floated several hundred feet to the rocky bottom. "Why don't you go get it?" Reed had chided Bruce. "It's just right there."

On the other side of the room sat Earl Sorenson. His face was long and glum and he didn't join in any of the levity. We all knew he was thinking of his horse, and as the fire crackled and the shadows danced on the walls, we respectfully left him to himself.

A surprise winter rain soaked us all the way down the canyon the next morning. It was miserably cold. Then, just before noon, the sun popped out and warmed everything but my frozen toes. Looking up from the back of my horse, I caught sight of a huge cave on the canyon rim. I wanted to climb up to it, but there was no time for such sidelines. We were cowboys on cowboy business, and that business didn't, and never does, include sightseeing. Uncle Ferrel, who did not consider himself a cowboy, had chosen to walk to the top of Mount Dellenbaugh that day and look for arrowheads. In a way I envied him.

Stretching my gaze to the south I searched for the mighty Colorado, knowing it was down in those snaky canyons somewhere. I thought that if I had gone with Uncle Ferrel to look for arrowheads on Dellenbaugh, maybe I could have seen the river from there. If I could see it, I thought, even just for a moment, it might pump some special feeling into me and make me stronger for the rest of the trip. The river never came into view, but soon plenty of cattle did, and that was all it took to reignite my adrenal glands.

> That ol' hoss he's a-gainin' right up on the ol' steer's tail,
> When ya hit a little clearin' ya let yer ol' rope sail.

Wild cattle everywhere. Judge lit into them like a coyote after a rabbit. There was nothing for me to do but hang tight and swing my rope. This was the day I learned what the old horse Judge was truly made of. He crossed the broken country with the moves of a half back. He jumped gullies like a deer and climbed ledges like a ram. He put me on a cow's tail and I roped the longhorn clean around the neck, then dallied and guided her around a tree just the way Reed had done it yesterday. Dad hopped off and tied my rope to the tree. Uncle Eldon rode in and scooped a loop under the cow's hind hooves and stretched her out while Dad tied a halter knot around her neck and nose.

With that one taken care of, we cornered another long-horned cow on the point of a rock. Her only way out was fifteen feet straight down. She glared at us, blowing snot and shaking the wide rack of horns on her head.

Those sharp horns found their target, opened up yer pony's side,
You was wishin' you could kill him before you got the ol' brute tied.

The cow made a run at us. Our horses veered away as her horns whisked by. She was free now and on the run. The chase began. Judge shot after her like a jet fighter from the deck of an aircraft carrier. We flew full tilt down the canyon behind the cow. I wound up my rope, swung, threw, and missed—wound, swung, threw, and missed again. We crashed through the brush and glided over the rocks—down country, further down country—until I knew at any moment we would topple into the Colorado River. My lungs began to burn, as if I were doing the running instead of the horse. Judge was winded as well and we both struggled to keep the chase alive. Finally Judge kicked in the afterburner and zipped me directly up to the cow's tail. This time the loop fit. The rope twanged taut as a violin string and we brought the wild cow to a halt. Dust floated around us like an eerie dream and I gasped for air. Judge's giant heart boomed between my legs.

Eldon suddenly appeared to help me out of the mess. The day had grown into a blaze; the sun beat down heavily now. By the time we pulled the cow back to the main herd my toes had completely thawed, sweat had broken out all over me, and my throat was as dry as the Twin Canyon Wash. Eldon smiled as we worked our way back up the canyon. "I was riding with Lew Black on a summer day years ago," Eldon said with a twinkle in his eye. "It was hotter than Hades. Me and Lew were out of water and we were a good two hours from a drink. You know what he up and said as we rode along that afternoon? Right out of the blue the old boy says, 'Ice cold Pepsi Cola sure would taste good right now.' I could have shot him dead right there."

Steaks awaited us back at the ranch. The stories were thick as those steaks that evening, and like the food, the stories kept coming until well after midnight.

We awoke the next morning to the most eye-opening sight of the expedition. A brilliant layer of snow stretched like a wide, soft bridal veil across the Wildcat flat. It was as if we had been reborn in a new country. We branded cattle in the mucky corral that morning, doctored Earl Sorenson's faltering horse, and prepared to drive back home across what was now a very mucky Arizona Strip.

> You kin bet we both remember all those places that we've been
> Poppin' bushes down at Joe's Spring, and brandin' down in Twin.

There was plenty of time to think on the way home. I wondered how I would explain all this to the guys at school. How do you describe wild cattle flying across the landscape, a good horse carrying you like a science fiction space vehicle over the rocks and gullies and ledges? How do you make them understand what it's like to rub shoulders with real cowboys like Reed Mathis and Buster Esplin who handle horses and cattle with a mystic sixth sense, or what it feels like to sit in a fire-warmed room on a couch and hear stories that stand your neck hair on end? And how do you explain something like lying alone under a juniper after dark, looking into the eyes of a suffering horse, and wishing you had something to eat?

I soon came to realize that there was no way I could make them see it, or feel it, or know it. I would simply go back to my spelling tests and kickball recesses and keep it all to myself like a treasure. For a fleeting moment I had *felt* how it might have been to be part of those stories of the Arizona Strip. Yet I sadly gave in to the fact that no matter how many books I read, or how many stories I hear, or how many trips I take, I will never know the Strip the way the originals did.

You had to be there.

A couple of weeks later we got word Earl Sorenson's horse had died.

Oh Lord! I've often wondered, and I've said a little prayer,
That those ol' ponies are grazin' in horse's heaven way up there.

U ƎK U

. . . Not a word

passes between Afton and William now. Thing is, the old boy is livid, and William can feel as much. Nothin' quieter than two speechless men headin' into Burnt Canyon. It's another world down in that country. Two fellas alone on their own planet.

Afton tops a ridge and stops to survey the situation. William rides up alongside, hoping to break the ice. He unzips that little fanny pack of his and pulls out a couple of apples. Reaches one toward Afton, who curtly looks the other way.

"Don't you carry a lunch?" William asks.

Afton cranks his chin back around. Inspects this William fella up and down, from the hiking boots to the faded-out pants to the T-shirt which is now fully exposed since he shed his overshirt. The T-shirt bears a strange looking emblem, a circle with a monkey wrench in it. Afton moans. His face flushes with disgust.

"I shoulda known you was one o' them environist types."

William's eyes widen. "You mean environmentalist," he says.

"I mean environist," Afton comes back.

"I don't know what an environist is," says William. "But I suppose I qualify as an environmentalist."

"I ain't personally met many environmentalists," Afton says, "but of those I've met, most of 'em lack the 'mental' part." . . .

8 Old Judge (1955–1976)

"He's a horse and you have to know what that is."

—Thomas McGuane

THERE ARE HORSEMEN in the region of Kazakhstan who hold four things sacred. In order of importance they are: their horse, their gun, their birthplace, and their wife. There have been times, I'm sure, when my mother would have considered Kazakhstan to be my Dad's kind of country.

I have an image of my father back in 1959, as he first sized up a brawny sorrel colt named Judge. Dad must have been like a sixteen-year-old kid, hesitating over the purchase of his first car: never mind it had no second gear, no registration, or that its front bumper was a little oversized. The important thing was that its chassis was tight, and that it ran. After all, buying a horse isn't much different than buying a used car: some things you might overlook, others can't be compromised under any condition. In the end, Dad got no lemon.

It turns out that Judge and I were born the same year. And we sort of grew up together. His sire was a classic quarter horse stallion named Copper Cloud, a son of Ed Echols. His mother was unregistered, the illegitimate daughter of Charlie and an American saddlebred mare.

Our local judge, LeRoy Cox, bred the horse, and that's where the name came from. Clayton Atkin, a respected area horseman and veteran cattleman of the Arizona Strip, bought the big-boned sorrel as a yearling, broke him, gelded him, and gave him his first lessons on the ranch.

It is true that no horse is without at least one fault, and before long Clayton discovered Judge's most unforgivable: the horse could not walk a step. Of course he could walk, but not the long-strided limber-clipping walk that cowboys look for. Judge was short that important gear between lazy amble and trot, the gear most preferred by range riders who spend the day in the saddle. Clayton decided to let the horse go.

I can see Dad now, leaning forward on Clayton's fence, his arms dangling over the top board, his awestruck eyes studying the stout, spirited gelding. He must have been as starry-eyed as the before-mentioned kid sizing up his first car, wistfully looking past the obvious flaws and seeing only a blazing sorrel with flaxen mane and tail—a tall, solid horse. Of course Dad had given him a test drive and knew for a fact that the horse couldn't travel. He also knew there were no papers on the animal. And he certainly could see that the gelding's head was one or two sizes too big for the rest of him.

But he must have dwelled on the positive points. The horse had everything else Dad was looking for. He was sound and smart. And he had heart. When Dad finally got to the bottom line he was willing to accept the trade-offs.

Dad paid four hundred dollars for Judge. That was a lot of money for a grade horse back in 1959. That kind of money could have bought a pile of tricycles, train sets, Tonka trucks, and BB guns for a wobbly little four-year-old kid. But Judge would eventually become infinitely more important in my young life than any toy ever could have.

Early on, before I ever got a chance to get on him, Dad caught the racing bug and matched Judge up with some of the fastest horses in southern Utah. The day he outran Bob Bowler's famous Billie by two lengths at Gunlock was the day Old Judge's legend began.

Dad rode him in all the gymkana events sponsored by the Washington County Sheriff's Posse in the early '60s. Each weekend during those winters he'd bring home a pretty trophy or two for some event like pole bending, ring racing, or the keyhole contest. Even Mom, a self-avowed nonhorse-person, began running barrels on Judge. That was when his suppressed dark side began to manifest itself.

From the beginning, Judge had been somewhat unpredictable, but Dad had no trouble channeling the horse's excess spirit toward positive outcomes. Mom, on the other hand, harbored a very real fear of Judge. She considered him to have come from some dark place, and Judge was keen to her jitters. When Mom was on him, if Judge didn't feel like ducking around the first barrel, he didn't. If he felt like running well, he did—which was quite often. If he decided to bag it, Mom didn't get a prize that day. It was Judge's choice. Mom was along mainly for the ride.

I started riding Judge when we were both six. Dad never let me ride him alone in those days. And he never told Mom about these rendezvous. I wasn't exactly afraid of the horse; let us simply say that I had a deep respect for him—a respect that bordered on terror. He pulled many stunts on me before I became a horseman. Yet I was proud that he never ran away with me, as he did with some of the other novices who got on him over the years. He taught me the horse-man quality of readiness—something they always tried to teach us in Boy Scouts but that can only really be learned in a true-life context such as that created between a boy and a horse. Judge taught me that dealing with an animal, like most of life's important undertakings, is no idle thing.

My earliest recollection of Judge's individual nature is the time Dad took him to Middleton, about seven miles from his home corral. There Dad left him in a rocky pasture along the base of a lava ridge where he could graze for a few weeks and build his feet up at little expense. That rocky pasture is now a ninehole, par-three golf course, driving range, and RV park. But at the time, Judge was apparently not impressed with the pasture's future real estate potential. He wanted out. He was deter-mined to leave and go home. After he shimmied through the barbed wire fence he took the straightest route to the barn—down St. George Boulevard. Dad got word of several sightings before he finally found Judge. The horse was standing at the gate of his home corral, waiting for someone to let him in. He had made the seven-mile return through downtown traffic unscathed.

During the fifteen years I knew him, Judge tried to leave me on sev-eral occasions. I have never believed that his escape attempts had any-thing to do with the way he felt about me; it seemed to me simply that there were times when he needed to get away.

One summer at the Panguitch rodeo I almost lost him forever. After the rodeo on Saturday night I tied him to the horse trailer which was parked on the infield of the race track surrounding the rodeo grounds. I didn't know that later in the night the rodeo stock contractor would turn his bucking horses onto the infield grass to graze.

When I came back the next morning I found a broken halter dangling from the lead rope still tied to the trailer. My rodeo buddies and I began a frantic search. A serious ache set into my chest. I had reached a point in my relationship with Judge where I didn't know what I'd do without him. Losing him then would have been akin to losing an eye, or a leg, or maybe even missing a meal.

A half-dozen of us scoured the rodeo grounds. No Judge. We had covered every corner of the rodeo complex when I finally noticed the stock contractor loading horses into a giant semi-trailer over behind the chutes. Immediately I spotted Judge in the runway. He was the sorrel standing nearly a neck above all the others—and he was headed up the ramp which led to the big stock trailer, which, ten minutes later, would have carried him out to the highway and all the way to Oakley, Utah.

"Hey, that's my horse!" I yelled at the rough looking guy who urged the horses up the ramp with a buggy whip.

"What the hell you talking about?" the man said. "These is company animals."

"That one right there is mine," I said. I pointed at Judge who had that "running-away-to-the-circus" look in his eyes.

"Looks like a bucking horse to me," the guy said.

"That's no bucking horse," I indignantly replied. "That's my rope horse, and I want him back."

The guy wasn't at all happy about having to run the horses back down the ramp. He uttered sharp words, the kind of words stock contractors have always been noted for using.

Another time, I was riding Judge along a rocky ledge of Paradise Canyon, about two miles from the corral. That ridge is now the west barrier of an on-again/off-again proposed golf course designed by the Arnold Palmer group. A trail cuts just below the summit of the ridge, and we followed it that day as we headed back to the corrals. I needed to stop and get off for a minute, so I stepped down onto the high side of the trail. As I swung out of the saddle there was a split second when I let go of the reins. Judge sensed the moment was coming and timed his getaway perfectly. He lit off, joyously kicking and snorting down the trail. I stood alone on the side of the ridge, finished what I had gotten off to do, and walked back to the corral.

I learned how to rope on Judge. We were both thirteen, and it was the summer the National Intercollegiate Rodeo Finals were held in St. George. The week of the finals Dad took me out to the Posse Grounds arena every morning and turned calves out for me. I must have chased twenty calves a day that week. I'd back into the box, untangle my rope, arrange the coils and the reins in my left hand, hold the loop high in my right hand, and nod. The calves were fresh, and shot from the chute like torpedoes. Judge exploded out of the box, and I clung to leather with all my strength, and we'd reach the other end of the arena before I could even begin to swing my rope. Usually, by the third lap, I was ready to throw. I'd let my loop fly and it would float aimlessly into the atmosphere and land somewhere well outside the calf's neighborhood.

Judge was patient, though. He'd scoot me in for another toss, for another air loop. After ten rounds of this my arm began to ache. But Dad kept saying, "One more," and after a half-dozen One Mores he would notice the tears beginning to form in my eyes, and we'd put the stock away and unsaddle and head down to the Sun Bowl for the afternoon performance of the college national finals.

It was hot that summer—even hotter than normal. The concrete Sun Bowl seats were so hot people were buying ice cubes and putting them under formica boards to sit on. We sweated out hour after hour watching the likes of Phil Lyne and A. C. Ekker do their stuff. It was so hot in Utah's Dixie that year the college national finals opted to move north to Bozeman, Montana, the next summer. They never came back.

As uncomfortable as that rodeo was, it pumped me full of vision and innoculated me with enough inspiration to keep me practicing my roping for a long time. In the months that followed I must have ridden Judge at least five days a week. When school started, my best friend Les Bracken and I started riding the Gunlock bus out to the northwest end of town and hopping off near the drive-in movie. We'd walk on over to the the Posse Grounds arena where our horses were stabled and practice roping until dark. It was Les's dad, LaVar Bracken, who taught me the finer points of competitive roping. He was one of the most successful rodeo ropers in southern Utah at the time, in spite of the fact that he'd lost part of his right tumb and half his index finger between the rope and the saddle horn in two separate roping accidents. LaVar and Les had a long line of great arena horses—Flicka and Ginge and April Lady among them, but even they would resort to using Judge for specific events in specific situations, just as I often borrowed their horses when certain needs arose. My cousin Brent also roped with us during those years. He rode Uncle Eldon's old legend of a horse named Tony, an animal cut from the same mold as Judge, just a couple of sizes larger.

We rode most every day after school and we had a lot of fine teachers. Among the best of them was Connie Bowler, southern Utah's leading horse trainer, who would often ride by on a colt he was working and teach us the finer points of reining or how to keep a pleasure class horse on lead. We didn't realize it then, but we were fortunate to be surrounded by good horses and fine horsemen. As the writer Thomas McGuane once put it: "The fragility of horses helps us see the difference between what is there in flesh and what is there in spirit. Men who have spent their lives with horses remember those spirits perfectly, and in that distinction lies an intimation of mortality that makes stockmen of every kind powerful company."

During those years of my initiation to the arena, Judge became my calf roping horse, heading horse, heeling horse, hazing horse, barrel racing, pole bending, keyhole, ring race, water race, flag race and boot race horse. He was even my 4-H show horse.

I washed him, brushed him, roached him and trimmed him. I painted his hooves with black shoe polish for the halter class, snipped his whiskers with Mom's best sewing scissors, combed his tail with a rake, and even sanded down the corky chestnuts on the insides of his front legs.

Judge did more and had more done to him than any horse I ever knew. He hunted deer, tracked wild cows, ran anchor in the pony express relay race at the Iron County Fair, dragged unmarked calves to the branding fire, ran match races, herded cows over Clover Mountain. Ethan Bundy and Brent Atkin even bulldogged on him—once. And the horse carried two of my cousins to rodeo queen titles. He was the kind of horse you might see one day out near the headwaters of the Beaver Dam Wash dodging the horns of a wild-eyed cow, and the next day galloping elegantly around the Las Vegas Convention Center arena in the Miss Rodeo America Pageant. One day he'd carry a seventy-pound kid around the 4-H pleasure class ring, and the next, pack a two hundred-pound buck off the side of Jackson Peak.

The horse was well cared for, but the best care in the world couldn't protect him from pain. He carried scars on every part of his frame and walked away from two major automobile wrecks that left the trailers he was riding in utterly demolished.

He was there through all my best times, all my changes. But there is no memory stronger than that cold February morning when I was fourteen years old. Old Judge carried me through the darkness that morning. The sun was just waiting to break over the Arizona Strip. He carried me out through the ponderosas at Mokiak and off the rim into an arm of Twin Canyon. The morning brightened and the air warmed and the Grand Canyon sprawled gloriously before us.

Sitting atop old Judge I felt a most pure sense of security. The kind of security one horse in a thousand offers. I wondered at his ability to pick his way down the trail, at the sheer strength and delicate grace all bound up in one being.

Later we broke into cattle—wild, thundering cattle—and Judge cut loose in hot pursuit. He ducked around rocks, slithered through brush, and lunged over gullies. Beneath me I felt a mystic combination of power and wisdom, raw might funnelled into precision. I felt courage and pride and integrity. And when I should have thought that I had asked everything possible of the horse, I slapped him across the rump with my rope and he gave it all to me again.

I have often considered the thought that there is no greater biological compilation of strength, endurance, intelligence, ability, and grace than that comprised in the fragile being of a good horse. Judge was one of them.

We both turned 21 in 1976. My life was just beginning. But that was the year we lost Old Judge.

... AFTON SITS UP
on that ridge atop ol' Nunya for some twenty minutes tryin' to work up the
nerve to head down into Burnt. William's got no choice but to sit there, and
as long as he's sittin' he's gonna ask questions.

"Why is it that cattlemen have such a distaste for environmentalists?"
William asks.

Afton sits stone-stiff, lookin' straight on. Then all of a sudden he cuts
loose.

"You got your eco-systems and your bio-diversity and all that fancy-
pancy stuff," Afton says. "What I wanna know is where's us human beings
supposed to fit in all of it? We've got ourselves to look out for, too," he says.
"Cowmen, we wanna produce. You environists, all you wanna do is pre-
serve. Hell, this country don't produce nothin' anymore. We buy it from
somebody else—like the Japanese who've got the gumption to produce and
make something out of their resources. All we do in this here country-'tis-of-
thee is paperwork. Everybody's got a job shuffling papers—writin' down
rules and regulations for everybody else. Most everybody you see nowadays
works for the government. Nobody wants to produce anymore, just pass
what we've got back and forth. How long do you think that can last? Some-
where, somebody's gotta produce. That meat don't just grow out the bottom
of the supermarket freezer. The leather for those shoes you wear don't just
drop out of the sky. How we gonna shelter ourselves? Can't cut down no
trees. How we gonna protect ourselves when the producing countries decide
if we ain't gonna do nothin' with our resources, they will?"

William's got a snicker on his face. He's gettin' a kick out of watching the
ol' cowboy philosopher work himself into a frenzy. "Easy now," says Will-
iam. "I'm not the enemy. I'm just a journalist."...

9   Max and Brandy

You could always count on seeing Max Cannon at the 24th of July rodeo in Enterprise. I used to look forward to a good visit with him there every summer—back in the days before he saddled old Brandy for the last time and rode into a storm.

At the bottom edge of the Escalante Desert (which should not be confused with the Escalante country over around the town of Escalante, and which isn't really a desert at all since deep water wells accessed by mega-horsepower electric pumps turned it into one of the finest tracts of farmland in the state) it would nearly always rain at rodeo time. One year after I had done well in the bareback bronc riding event, I worked my way up into the stands to visit with Max. He flashed me a wide grin as I stepped up the bleachers toward him. When he smiled, his substantial glasses raised a little on his nose. "Dandy ride," he said.

"Thanks," I replied. "How are things on the farm?"

"Good," Max said. He was a unique blend of farmer and rancher, proficient at both in a day and age when folks usually specialized in one or the other.

"And Brandy?" I asked

"He's gettin' old, but still good as ever." Max talked softly. You had to sit close to catch every word.

That was the night a summer storm broke loose over Enterprise that wanted to crack your mind open. About the time the rodeo got over, thunder started rumbling across the Escalante Desert like roaring chariots, and before the parking areas had cleared, lightning was zapping in every direction. When we came back for the next night's performance, a dead bull lay in a pasture out behind the arena. The bolly-faced

Hereford lay on his side, stiff as rawhide, legs sticking straight out. He was an old curved-horned bull and he hadn't moved since the moment a million volts hit him the night before.

First time I met Max Cannon I was twelve years old. It was out in southeastern Nevada, on the west side of the Beaver Dam Slope where Dad and other cattlemen wintered their cattle. We met at the Upper Well, there where it sits at the foot of Lime Mountain in the bottom of the Bull Valley Wash. I met a lot of fine cowboys there, but none finer than Max.

Dad had taken me out of school in mid-May for the Drive. This was the ultimate for a wide-eyed kid who hated school and loved the thought of being a cowboy. He introduced me to all the real cowboys that first May morning and each of them was kind enough to acknowledge me in some small way, but Max seemed the most friendly. When he shook my hand I felt an extra squeeze, a reassuring gesture that pumped some confidence into me. I couldn't see into Max's eyes because he wore strong dark glasses; he always wore them in daylight. He had a roundish face and he carried a lot of gold in his teeth. His smile came across big and warm, even if you couldn't see his eyes. And he almost whispered when he talked. I suppose a lifetime of hollering at cows had worn his vocal chords thin and he was probably trying to ration what was left for the thirty or so good years of life that should have remained on his calender.

A coffee pot simmered on the fire down in the bottom of that rocky canyon. Some of the cowboys puffed cigarette smoke into the warm air while the week's plan was laid out in the dirt. They talked of places like The Burn and Bracken Pond and Cedar Wash. This was winter range, which meant it got awful hot once spring slipped away. As the morning grew into midday, flies began to buzz around the cowboys and sweat started to show through their shirts. They talked for a long time. Apparently it was a complicated planning process. I watched Max through this whole ceremony and noticed that he was a good listener. He seldom opened his mouth, yet when he did, the others listened intently. Max didn't waste words.

During the long chats around the fire over the next few days I noticed how Max kept an eye on the handsome yellow gelding tied to his truck. The horse's name was Brandy. He was a fine-bred quarter horse with a good disposition and a lot of cow in him. One afternoon as we rode out to gather cattle, Max hooked up with Dad and me. We cut up a draw and topped out along a rolling blackbrush flat that looked to stretch on for miles. Behind us the jagged ridge of Lime Mountain muscled high out of the bleak landscape and stood tall and sharp against a hot blue sky. That razorback hump of gray rock stood so high above the surrounding landscape that even at several miles distance you were forced to cock your neck to focus on its summit. The mountain stands alone in the wilderness. It is a stark and fitting monument to the cowboys and their horses who've spent lifetimes trailing around it.

I watched Max and Brandy twist through the brush that afternoon. Max sat the yellow horse like an able knight. The two moved as one. Brandy walked out smart and smooth, and Max reined him with only a subtle flick of his fingers. Dad was on Hector and I rode Judge. I envied the smooth ride Dad and Max got from their mounts. Judge had never learned to walk and to keep up with the others required a tooth-jarring trot.

"How you and ol' Judge gettin' along?" Max asked as I trotted up alongside Brandy.

"Fine," I said, still not feeling well-enough acquainted to carry on much of a conversation.

"These two horses are brothers, you know," said Max. "They're both Copper Cloud colts."

"I didn't know that," I said. "Wish this one could walk like yours."

"Now there's the thing about horses," Max said. "You never get one that can do it all. You get one that turns on a dime, but then he don't know a cow from a coyote. Or you get one that works cows like a dream, such as these here Copper colts, and maybe he doesn't keep worth a dang. Take ol' Judge there," Max went on, "so he *can't* walk. Well, I've seen him outrun the fastest horses in the county. He's as good an all-around horse as you're gonna find. And then you take Brandy here. He walks out nice and he handles cattle as well as you could ever ask a horse to. But he don't have near the speed that one does. Ol' Judge there'd leave him in the dust."

"Right now I'd sooner he could walk than run," I said.

The rest of the day we visited at length while we looked for cattle. Max asked me about school, about girls, about what I wanted to be when I grew up. He told me about all the horses he'd owned—the good ones and the ones that didn't last—about chasing mustangs, about his grandsons Fred and Kevin, and about farming out on the desert north of Enterprise.

I saw Max often after that. He summered his cattle up on the Acoma allotment and he'd stop in at Clover Valley to visit when he came through. Brandy was always in the back of the truck when he drove up. He'd unload the horse, run him some water, and pour him a nose-bag of grain. Whenever I rode with Max I watched how perfectly he and Brandy worked together. I got to liking the horse as much as I did Max.

After I went away to college I didn't see Max Cannon for a long time. Years later we visited again at the Enterprise Rodeo and that was the last time I saw him. He sold his Acoma permit to my Dad and the Hafen Brothers, and spent most of his last days at the farm on the Escalante Desert growing hay, keeping a cow or two, and raising fine horses.

Late one summer night after my wife and I had been to a movie the phone rang. It was Dad, long distance. He said he had bad news. I braced for the worst.

"It's about Max Cannon," Dad said. I detected an uncommon crack in his voice.

"He was riding near his farm yesterday. A thunderstorm came in and he was too far out to make it back. Lightning . . ." Dad stopped for a moment. He swallowed hard and finished the sentence. "Lightning hit him. They found him lying next to his horse. Both of them dead."

I didn't say anything for a long time. Then, finally, I asked Dad the only question I knew he could answer. "What horse was he on?"

"You know as well as I do what horse he was on," Dad said.

. . . IT'S HIGH NOON
on the edge of Burnt Canyon and Afton ain't finished his sermon. Sittin' on
the back of ol' Nunya like that, clouds gathering above, he's in a good position to save the world. And William seems content to listen.

"All these backpackers come out here bad-mouthin' me 'cause there's cows
on the range," grumbles Afton. "I tell 'em, 'Hey, if there wasn't people tryin'
to produce something off the land, people like you wouldn't have the leisure
ner the wherewithal to recreate on it.' There was a time when everybody
spent a good part of their day just seein' to their daily bread. But nowadays
it's all placed before 'em on a silver platter, so there's plenty of time to join
groups and look for things to bellyache about—plenty of time to get out into
nature, commune, so to speak, and get all bent out of shape 'cause somebody
had the audacity to turn a cow loose in the same spot where they wanted to
sit down and eat their bean sprouts for lunch.

"They've got this notion that they're gonna save us all by kicking cows off
the public lands. Maybe nobody would notice if all us cowboys up and died
tomorrow. But I'll guaran-dang-tee you one thing, what we've got here is an
awfully frightening trend. They're concerned about the turtles and the owls
and the minnows, but what about the mothers and the fathers and the children? They want to do away with the steel mills, get rid of the power plants
and the factories. They want the loggers out of the forests, the hunters out of
the hills, and they want us cowboys off the ranges. The way things are goin',
they'll get rid of us all eventually, but it sure as hell won't be pretty when
they do. What they'll have is a big pristine wilderness and no wherewithal
to enjoy it. Thing is, the only reason they've got the time and luxury to be
so-called environmentalists now is because there was a time when us Amer-
icans were willing to produce." . . .

10   Last of the Homesteaders

THE WEATHER UP near the headwaters of Beaver Dam Wash was so far out of whack that spring of 1984, Ross Mathews figured the government must have had something to do with it. It was the white-haired cowboy's seventy-eighth spring and he'd seen nearly all of them at close range—right there where the Mathews Place hugs the Utah–Nevada line, just below Beaver Dam State Park.

As we dropped into the juniper-studded canyon I wondered what ever drew anyone here in the first place. It was hard country. The kind of country you'd have to truly care about to stay. When we hit the bottom of the canyon and came onto Mathews property, it began to dawn on me why someone might want to come here, and how he might never want to leave.

Ross Mathews was born a Nevadan and remained one all his life. But that was not his original destiny. His great grandfather Charles Mathews was a Mormon pioneer sent by Brigham Young to settle in southern Utah. Somewhere up along the Utah Trail his party took a wrong turn and ended up in Panaca, Nevada. Once there, they decided to stay, and that's where Ross was born in the early spring of 1906.

My father first took me down to the Mathews Ranch for a visit when I was thirteen. Ross was beginning to show his age even then. I remembered him as a thin, stooped man who offered the appearance that most every bone in his body had been broken at one time or another. His face was the texture of rawhide, drawn up and wrinkled, yet it was easy to imagine that he had once been a handsome young man. His wife, Orma, always had her hair in a bun fastened close to her head. She had an elderly, honorable countenance about her, yet she seemed young and agile next to Ross. They had invited us in for a visit that night long ago. The visit stretched into supper, and then, as the evening slipped quickly away, they offered us bunks to spend the night. That being a slower and simpler time, Dad and I decided to stay. There was no one back at the ranch to miss us. That night was my introduction to authentic cowboy hospitality, an art that we're losing—not so much because people are changing, but because the right circumstances, such as available time, simply don't exist anymore.

Now, as we came back again, there would be another evening of talk and good food, and maybe we'd even spend the night. Ross greeted us at the gate. He looked like a stick figure caricature from an Old West cartoon. His hat was crumpled and soiled, and his face scrunched when he smiled. We parked and went inside the warm house, a handsome little bungalow sitting above a pond with ducks. The talk began immediately and continued well into the night.

Ross had grown up in Clover Valley with my grandmother, and he had plenty to tell us about those days. They had both gone to school and church in the same one-room, clapboard building with a cast-iron bell in a steeple above the door. Ross recounted several stories about Grandma, and he told us more of his own history. His grandfather, William Mathews Sr., and his own father, William Jr., had been freighters and casket makers in Panaca. "They built real nice caskets the way I remember 'em," Ross said proudly. "They were wagon makers too, wheelrights, and pretty handy with their hands. That's run right down through the family. You can see it in my boys." You could see it all around the Mathews Ranch. Every fence on the place was in good repair. The barn stood solid over a nice stack of hay. The workshop was full of well-maintained machinery, and the beautiful little house sat rather stately down beyond. Everything was thoughtfully laid out, well kept, even after all the kids had long since moved to town, leaving Ross and Orma to handle most of the work themselves.

Ross had no plans for retirement. The word did not exist in his vocabulary. Nor had he any plans to move to town, even though he and Orma owned a home in St. George, some seventy miles away. "I'm like the old cow that's accustomed to her range," Ross chuckled. "Once she knows the country, it's hard to pull her off it."

Orma felt the same way. When the children were young, she spent winters in St. George where they could go to school. But now she stayed year-round with Ross at the ranch. "To learn about man," Orma said that night, "you go to the city. To learn about God, you go to the wilderness." Orma seemed to be much more interested in God. And, I figured, this was about as close to wilderness as anyone could get on a full-time basis. Over the years, they had succeeded in making the place a peaceful and comfortable haven. Volumes of guest books on the mantle over a rock fireplace testified to the Mathews blend of hospitality.

Yet hospitality is not what you would expect as you approached the main ranch gate which was preceded by a volley of "No Trespass–Keep Out" signs. Ross was the best kind of friend if he knew you and trusted you. But if he didn't know you, or if you hadn't been sent by someone he knew, you were lumped in with a world full of potential vandals.

Ross had built a mock grave alongside the road near the main gate; it was a mound of dirt with boots poking out the bottom and a grave marker bearing the words: "He Won't Trespass Anymore." It was not the warning of an antisocial recluse, but simply a sad message from a family plagued by vandals and thieves over many decades. It was a message to those with guilty hearts, but to friends it was nothing more than a light-hearted conversation piece.

Sitting in his chair by the popping fire, Ross clasped his time-worn hands over his knees and mulled back over his childhood. "I was ten when we moved to Clover Valley," he recalled. "That was in 1916, and we lived at the homestead up near the east end of the valley." Ross had started school in Panaca and was ready to enter the fifth grade when the family moved to Clover Valley. But they didn't happen to offer fifth grade at the Clover Valley school that year, so Ross took the fourth again. "I took the fourth grade twice and that's how I got so damned smart," he said.

"Up until I was fifteen, I was just a little runt, ninety-six pounds," he said. "That winter I went trapping with my friend Jimmy Dobbins and I started growing up. I guess it was all those beans and venison and mountain scenery."

He got his true education that winter, and in the process became well acquainted with the upper Beaver Dam Wash drainage, where he would one day make his home and earn his living. Ross Mathews and Jimmy Dobbins caught coyotes, bobcats, grey fox, and the biggest striped skunk that ever waddled through the Beaver Dam Wash. "But it was no money-making proposition," Ross recalled. "I think we got five dollars for a coyote hide, two-fifty for bobcat, and maybe a buck-fifty for grey fox. If it hadn't been for the folks grubstaking us, we'd have never made it."

Looking around the Mathews living room I got the feeling there was more to Ross Mathews than you generally attribute to a cowboy. Shiny, full arrowheads were embedded in the fireplace mantle, along with ancient manos and metates. A variety of head gear hung on the deer antler rack, from soiled baseball caps to battered cowboy hats. Piles of books and magazines lay in clusters around the room. A well-used *Book of Mormon* lay on top of one stack. Years later, at his funeral, family members vouched for Ross's testimony of the book and how he read from it regularly all his life. During his eighty-six years he attended formal church meetings only on rare occasions. Yet he practiced his religion daily and never denied his faith.

Over on a table lay a pile of glittering rocks next to a microscope. "He's always been a prospector," Orma said. Ross chuckled and shifted in his chair. "I started prospecting when I was ten," he said, and he went on to explain in detail the geology of the area in his own layman's way. He had a little sparkle in his eye, that magic gleam that draws the prospector on toward the big strike. "It's kinda hard for a cowboy to be a prospector," he continued. "You tend to lose track of the cows when you spend all your time looking at the ground. The only reason most cowboys pick up a rock is to throw it at a cow."

Ross said when he was very young his father went off to make some cash drilling wells, leaving Ross to tend the cows and take care of the chores. "There was no place for bums or loafers in those days," he said.

"But I was able to sneak away once in a while and wander the hills to look for pretty rocks."

"We also handled the mail in Clover Valley all through the years until 1943. I made twenty-five or thirty dollars a month at it. But it was awful hard work and time consuming." He'd meet the train three days a week. It would be anywhere from on time to twelve hours late. "I'd hate to know how many hours of my life were spent standing there next to the tracks waiting for that train," he said.

Ross was twenty-eight years old when he met Orma. That was in 1934, and she was twenty at the time. She had come from St. George with a friend to a Civilian Conservation Corps party. Ross happened to come too. He was up in a tree picking pinenuts when the branch he was on snapped and he landed at Orma's feet. "She still gets a kick about how I fell for her," Ross joked. He truly did. They were married the next year. "I ain't been able to trade her off since," he chuckled.

The couple spent the early part of their marriage at Clover Valley— long enough for their oldest child to attend first grade in the one-room church-school where Ross had gotten that extra year of fourth grade. Later they moved to their place on the upper extremities of the Beaver Dam Wash and obtained about half of what is now 450 acres through the Desert Entry Program. The rest of their private land came through trades and purchases over the years. After they took up residence on the Wash, Orma began moving to St. George during the winters, taking the children to school there. But Ross never went to town much. He preferred to ride out even the hardest winters right there at the ranch, even though it meant being alone and out of communication with the world. There was one winter when the old horse he called Chub threw his head back and broke Ross's arm. Ross promptly made a splint out of a Mother's Oats carton, got back on the horse, and rode through the bitter winter to Acoma, some ten miles away.

"As the swelling went down, I'd cinch the carton a little tighter," Ross said. From Acoma he caught a ride to Chet Oxborow's place in Caliente, and Chet flew him in a private plane to St. George where he got proper medical attention.

Ross had already learned his lesson about getting proper medical attention back in the early 1940s. He had been riding near Bunker Pass one day when his horse started to show off. "He whirled back and went to bucking and I landed on the seat of my pants," Ross said. "Split my pelvis and hip." He struggled back on the horse, which was his only alternative if he was to ever get back home again, and rode until dark. The next morning he got up, climbed on his horse, did his day's work, and stuck to his normal routine for a week.

"Finally it got to the point where I didn't feel like getting off the horse," Ross recalled. "I was crippled, and I was too stubborn to go to the doctor." He suffered from the injury for years, until one day he finally broke down, went to town, and had a new hip installed.

"I've had ribs broke, shoulders broke, arms broke," Ross said. "Hell, do I have to confess all my stupidity?" He grunted as he shifted in his chair. "That's the problem with being alone," he went on. "When you go off a horse, the only thing you can do is get back on again." Then he smiled. "Most of my accidents happened when a horse went down on me. I was as good as anybody at riding a pony right into the ground."

The ground he rode was generally government ground. He spent his life on the public ranges, or on private islands in a sea of public domain. His encounters with government administrators were often combative, the result of a practical, independent individual attempting to deal with a complex, bureaucratic system.

"Those early settlers had their problems," Ross said. "But they had a picnic compared to what we've been through with the government."

Ross always spoke his mind to land administrators. He had a brash way of showing his teeth. "Most of the time I might as well have been talking to a tree," he said. "Those government people can pass the buck so far you'll never find it. There's no such thing as a straight answer from them boys."

Ross Mathews practiced what he considered his own brand of environmentalism over the years. He claimed he never overgrazed the land he leased from the government, and swore that the range today is in better shape than it was when he was a boy. "It's not so much a matter

of how many cows you run," he said. "It's where you put 'em, and
when, and how much rain you get. You've got to remember, this is
desert country. We're not talking about Montana grasslands. Believe it
or not, there's plenty of good feed here for cattle, and if we don't use it,
it's a resource wasted."

Ross Mathews lived long enough to face the modern environmental
movement head-on. He regarded the federal land legislation of the
1970s and '80s—along with the ensuing lists of regulations—as a sign
of the times. He figured it was mostly the result of too many people
with too little to do. "The man who lives on the land and tries to make
something of it is now the villain," he said. "Those who sit at desks and
dream up regulations and don't produce a damned thing, they're considered the good guys."

Little of what came out of Washington during the '70s and '80s
made sense to Ross. He considered himself a steward of the land. But as
the years passed, he began to feel the modern world tighten around him
as more and more government, more and more paperwork, more and
more land managers encircled his long established way of doing things.

Ross's feelings and beliefs regarding the land were tied to his
upbringing—therefore, to his religion. He believed it was wrong for a
healthy, strong-bodied man not to pull his own weight. It was wrong,
as far as he was concerned, not to harvest in the most productive way
possible those natural and renewable resources which God had made
available. He also believed that his stewardship meant judicious and
wise use. He did not consider himself an abuser of the land as today's
critics might call him, but a caretaker of it.

"Nowadays it's just fashionable to be one of these environmentalists," he said. "They want the cattle off the ranges, the loggers out of
the forests, the miners out of the hills. I've got no problem with being
concerned about the environment; I've been concerned about it all my
life, but there's something morally wrong with a country when a certain species of plant or animal gets more concern than an unborn child.
We're in a decline here—a moral decline that could truly foul things up
if we don't wake up."

These were thoughts which Ross had formed from his own experience and reading, with no television entering into the equation. It was obvious that he had spent hours during long winters alone considering such issues.

For years Ross carried a sidearm. He claimed it was to keep the jackrabbits in check. But it was always there if he needed it for anything else, such as protecting his private property, or maybe to help strengthen his hand in conversations with government land administrators.

There were those who tried to blame Ross and others like him for the decline in deer numbers in his region. But Ross had his own theory about what happened to the deer. "We used to have a large deer population," Ross recalled. "Interestingly enough, that was when we were running the most cattle. You've got to realize that cattle and deer complement each other. Cattle help keep the brush country open, and when you develop water holes for cattle, you're doing the same for the deer. But the fact is, we had deer die by the hundreds back in the 1950s when they were doing all that atomic testing over the hill there at Mercury. I'm telling you, that fallout had something to do with it."

In spite of his run-ins with the government, Ross was still running about sixty head of cattle on the range near his home. They carried the Quarter-Circle-X Diamond-X brand on their ribs. And Ross and Orma still grew most everything they needed right there on the place: peaches, pears, plums, apples of many varieties, vegetables, and even some strawberries. Ross still puttered with the machinery out in the shop, building and repairing. And you had to believe that on a slow day he would head down the wash and work his way up a draw, kick over a few rocks—still searching for that elusive vein and thinking back over the good days.

"When I was young," Ross mused just before we all retired to bed that night, "I thought I wanted to be a pilot. When I saw a plane in the sky I dreamed of flying away. But the older I got, the closer to the ground I wanted to stay."

For the rest of his life he kept his feet on the ground, on the very land that sprouted him, and though he would've liked to have had more education, he learned all there was to know about the life he chose to keep. "If I get ten miles from this place, I'm lost," he said.

The world whizzed by, and Ross kept his feet firmly planted.

"No regrets," he said. "But I've always questioned my own sanity. You don't have to be crazy to be a cowboy, but it damned sure helps."

On February 1, 1992, at the age of 85, Ross Mathews died. He was sitting in a rocking chair near the fireplace at his home up below the headwaters of the Beaver Dam Wash.

. . . *"YOU EVER BEEN hungry?" Afton asks William. William's sittin' on a rock now, holding the reins attached to Nothin's bridle and gazing down into Burnt with a grave look on his face.*

"Of course I've been hungry."

"I mean really hungry," Afton comes back. "I mean so hungry you'd consider infringing on somebody else's rights just to get something to eat."

"I can't say I've ever been that hungry," says William.

"Ain't many people who have," says Afton. He still sits atop Nunya with the stern posture of a general. "Not in this country, anyway; not in this land of plenty."

Afton pauses for a good thirty seconds. One of those pauses for effect that all good orators use. William's on the edge of his rock.

"Three days," says Afton, finally. "I figure at any given moment we're about three days from big changes. Three days without food and you wouldn't have no more environists. Three days without food and all of a sudden everybody'd be scrambling—be producing again. No more paper work. Just good old-fashioned hand-to-mouth, sweat-of-your brow work. We'd all be planting crops and grazing cows and concerning ourselves with the basics again.

"The way I figure it, as long as people got plenty to eat, us cowboys ain't gonna be heroes no more." . . .

11   Becoming a Hand

CLARK HOUSTON USED to be a barber. He cut my hair when I was a kid. He gave me good standard cuts while all my friends were letting their hair grow long like John Lennon's. The thing I remember most about haircuts at Clark's place on the Boulevard downtown was a picture framed on the wall. It was one of those ancient color calendar paintings in a metal frame behind glaring glass. In it an old cowboy had just dismounted and was standing next to his horse relieving himself. It was not a full frontal view, of course, but what the cowboy was doing was obvious. Off in a corner of the picture, next to a bush, the cowboy's dog was engaged in the same activity. "The Pause That Refreshes," read the caption below the picture.

I began getting haircuts at Clark's even before I could read; so, as the years passed, the picture on the wall increased in meaning. Clark never said anything about it. It just hung there while Clark snipped and hummed—a subtle little slice of life that communicated something about the barber to the person sitting in the chair. Now, all these years later, I realize that Clark must have spent much of the day during his barbering years floating somewhere in that picture on the wall. It had all the elements of escape he must have longed for, cooped up in that twelve-by-twelve shop, wading through piles of fluffy hair, snipping away hour after hour.

The way I remember it, the picture was set on the open range. The cowboy was dressed in denim pants, boots, chaps, and a cowboy hat. There was a horse, a rope hung over the saddle horn, and open country as far as you could see. That picture, crude and silly as it might have seemed to some, must have been Clark's window to the future.

After I got into high school I started going to style salons for my haircuts. The barbering business must have really dropped off during that era. That must have been about the time Clark got out of it. He made the natural transition to real estate. And real estate became his springboard into the cattle business—the place he was headed all along.

Clark did well in real estate. Well enough to stake himself a ranch. And once he rode off into the sunset of his own range, he never looked back. He had reached the "pause that refreshes" stage of life. In the years since he turned in his scissors for a saddle I have never heard him mention the word haircut.

To become a "cowman" you simply buy a setup. To become a "cowboy," as Clark learned, requires some credits toward the degree. Dad took on our former family barber as an apprentice and they are still in the schooling process. Clark has come a long way—an awful long way from that twelve-by-twelve cubical on the Boulevard. He's learned to handle cows with finesse, learned when to move them from one pasture to the other, when to wean, when to doctor, how to keep them fat and sell them right. He can ride twenty miles in a day and grind out another twenty the next. He has earned his first degree.

Dad bestowed that degree one day a couple of years ago. It was on Clark's birthday. Dad picked him up before dawn at his home near the golf course in Bloomington Hills. "Let's go get your birthday present," Dad said as Clark jumped in the truck.

"What's it gonna be?" Clark asked.

"It's a surprise," Dad said. "Be patient now."

My Dad, though terminally impatient with livestock, possesses an uncanny ability for patience when it comes to telling a story, getting to the punch line, or pulling off a stunt like the one he had planned for this day. Clark figured Dad was going to take him out to the corrals and hand him a new bridle, or a sack of horse feed, or maybe something like an adopted mustang or a jackass fresh off the shores of Lake Mead. But Dad didn't stop at the corrals. And it was too early to stop at the feed store, or any other store for that matter. Clark was going to get his birthday present somewhere outside the city limits—somewhere out in the hills. At least, that's where Dad was headed.

He drove all the way to Clover Valley, nearly two hours from Clark's front doorstep. The sun broke the skyline as they traveled, and they talked cows and horses all the way, with no more mention of a birthday present. Clark figured maybe his present was going to be a tour of the range. After all, for a cowboy there is nothing more rewarding than a leisure day surveying the countryside, checking the grass, and sizing up the herd.

Dad stopped at the ranch house and opened the saddle shed. He grabbed two chain saws, hefted them into the back of the pickup, and went back for a can of fuel and a bottle of oil. Still no explanation.

Clark played along. He knew it was no use trying to pry anything out of Dad. They got back into the truck and headed up the other side of the valley toward Bunker Peak. At the Rock Canyon turnoff they made a left toward the Simkins Chaining, Dad's favorite wood cutting area. A half mile this side of the loading chute corrals, Dad cut off the dirt road and drove out into the trees. He followed a rough trail that vaguely remained from previous passes, crunching brush and flipping tree branches off the rearview mirrors. Clark said nothing as Dad hummed a tune and wrestled the steering wheel.

Finally they reached the spot and Dad brought the truck to a rocking halt. "Here we are!" he said.

Clark gave him a "So what?" look.

"Let's get to work," Dad said. "You knock 'em down and I'll cut 'em up."

The rest of the morning, and into the afternoon, they cut dead juniper trees into firewood and loaded the entire jag into the pickup. Clark didn't ask questions and Dad offered no explanation. A load of wood would be nice, Clark figured. But he already had his firewood in for the winter, and he knew Dad knew it. He kept cutting and loading until the stock racks of the pickup brimmed with fresh-cut juniper logs.

They drove home sweat-soaked. Dad hummed most of the way and Clark accepted the fact that he was getting a load of wood, which he didn't really need, for his birthday—a load which he had helped cut and load at great physical expense. A load he would likely have to *unload* later that night.

When they arrived in town, Dad drove down Main Street, past the jeweler's, the florist's, the movies, and the new video arcade. He drove straight to Jolley's Western Wear on the corner of Main and Tabernacle, smack in the heart of the downtown business district. It was just about closing time. The Jolley Brothers, our town's long-time supplier of the cowboy uniform, came out directly.

"You got 'er, huh?" they said.

"She's all there," Dad said. "I'd say about a cord and a half. Is the trade still on?"

"You bet."

Dad turned to Clark, whose face was a giant question mark. "Well," Dad said, impatiently, "they're gonna close the place up if we don't hurry." They walked inside the store, and Dad led Clark straight to the wall covered with premium felt cowboy hats.

"Pick a hat, Clark. Any hat," Dad said. "The hat you choose is yours. Oh, and, Happy Birthday."

CI E K U

. . . THE SUN DUCKS
behind a gray cloud as Afton and William begin their descent into Burnt
Canyon. Those little dark clouds have been congregating now for an hour
or so. From off in the distance comes a low rumble of thunder and Afton
starts to perk up a bit.

On the other hand, William begins to show concern. "What if it rains?"
he asks.

"Then it rains," says Afton.

"Then what do we do?"

"Thank the Lord for small favors," says Afton. "You got any other sug-
gestions?"

"I didn't bring rain gear."

"Good," says Afton. "You bring rain gear and it never rains. At least this
way we've got a chance for some moisture." . . .

12   The Story behind the Smile

BACK WHEN OUR neighborhood sat on the fringe of civilization and there was plenty to do in the wild brush near home, Brad Jennings and I rode bikes for hours on hot summer days. Brad had the new Sting-Ray with a sissy bar rising two feet above the back of the seat. I rode a conventional Schwinn, nothing fancy, but it took me everywhere Brad's bike took him. We'd meander through the fields over well-beaten trails that wove among trees, down through gullies, and took us to the edge of our universe. We'd talk about baseball, model cars, space-ships, and cowboys. And we'd discuss our heroes: Mickey Mantle, Hoss Cartwright, Roy Rogers, and Sky King.

"My dad's a cowboy," I boasted to Brad one day.

"So," Brad said. "My grandpa was the best cowboy in all of St. George, Utah."

I knew my story was sound, but I wasn't so sure Brad was telling the truth.

A few years ago the Dixie Roundup celebration in St. George observed its fiftieth anniversary. During the weeks preceding the big event I began a project to identify some of the original cowboys who competed in those first rodeos back in the 1930s. I talked to men like Walter Shelley, Roy Kurt, Reed Mathis, and Dick Hammer. Each one told me his story, then asked me if I had talked to a man named Clyde McQuaid.

"Who's this Clyde McQuaid?" I asked my father one day.

"You know him," Dad said. "He lives on Tabernacle Street in the white house with the arched roof. You see him most every night during the summer out on the porch in his wheelchair."

"Oh, yeah," I said. "Sure, I've seen him. He's always wearing a cowboy hat."

"He's Brad Jennings' grandpa," Dad said. "A fine roper in his day."

So Brad wasn't a liar after all. Or was he? He said his grandpa was the best cowboy in all of St. George.

I went to the county library and began rolling through the old *Washington County News* microfilm—all the way back to 1935, November 14. In the report on the first Dixie Roundup I read the following:

Twelve hundred spectators, the largest crowd ever to attend a sports program in Dixie, turned out to the rodeo sponsored by the Lions Club, and run off under the direction of Robert Hurley, Armistice Day, November 11, at the city park . . .

I read on, following the column down to where it described the events, the excitement, the purses. Then I came to the results:

First place in bronco riding, Dick Lockett, with Roy Kurt and Walter
Shelly tied for second.

And then the discovery:

First place in calf roping, Clyde McQuaid.

Brad Jennings, I thought to myself, you are an honest man. I've got to meet your grandpa.

Dad went with me to see Clyde on a scalding July afternoon. Clyde's bubbly wife, Juanita, met us at the door and presented us to the old cowboy who sat slightly slumped in his wheelchair. He straightened right up when he saw us. There was a fan on a table next to him blowing like a windy day on the Arizona Strip. Clyde extended his left hand (the right one didn't seem to work) as we approached. When I shook his trembling warm hand I looked into his eyes and was lost there for a moment. I sensed pure kindness in his presence. I'd never felt quite that welcome anywhere before.

Clyde had on a fine looking straw cowboy hat. He wore a plaid western shirt with a bolo tie, gray slacks, and a lustery pair of black boots. He was slender and frail, and white as a cloud. His face bore sharp features, but most prominent was the slick, wide set of upper teeth in his mouth, and those sea-blue eyes that engulfed you like a wave each time you looked into them. Between those teeth and those eyes, Clyde McQuaid had a smile that could turn a snowbank into a puddle.

Mrs. McQuaid went into another room and we cowboys started talking rodeo. "When I was a kid," Clyde said slowly, "I wanted to be a cowboy more than anything in the world." He spoke softly and in a high voice. I moved a little closer to catch every word. "I think I wore out more lasso ropes than anybody." He paused and smiled between each sentence. "I had Lawrence McMullin for an idol, and I thought if I ever got as good as him I'd be all right."

Clyde told us he was born in Search Light, Nevada, and grew up in Leeds, Utah. "I always loved to rope," he said. "I left the bucking horses to Roy Kurt and Don Horn—let them do the twistin'." Clyde rocked in his wheelchair like Ray Charles at the piano. He was genuinely happy to be talking to us about the good old days. He spoke longingly of men like Walter Shelley, Jim Price, Lee Hafen, and Wallace Mathis—men he team roped with in his heyday.

One year, Clyde said, he was heeling for Walter Shelley at a rodeo in Mesquite, Nevada. They were getting beat awful bad, and their money was going fast. "I told Walter, 'Let's fill the truck with gas and get something to eat, that way if we don't do any good, we can at least get home.'" They bought gas, filled their stomachs, then went back to the rodeo and roped a steer in eighteen seconds flat. "We won a hunnerd and eighty bucks," Clyde said through his widest smile. "That was in the days when you could buy a sack of flour for four bits."

The conversation went on for over an hour. Clyde would tell a story, then smile big as life, tipping his head back to think of another. At one point he got so excited his left leg went into a spasm, trembling lightly at first, then it began shaking and jumping like a wounded rabbit. He tried to hold the leg steady with his hand, but it shook even more and finally went completely out of control. "Hit it," Clyde said to me.

"What?"

"Hit my leg."

I scooted over and tapped Clyde's knee. "No, hard," he said. I knocked it with my fist. "Harder!" With all the force I could muster, I whopped the top of Clyde's leg and suddenly the limb stopped dead.

Then Clyde told us how it had happened. That summer of 1946 he'd been working hard on the farm and he wasn't feeling well at all. But a little sickness wasn't going to keep Clyde McQuaid away from the July 24th rodeo at Enterprise. On the last night of the rodeo he was in first place in the wild cow milking event and the calf branding contest. When it came time for the calf roping (his best and favorite event) he had begun to feel downright sick. He went ahead and competed, roped the calf cleanly, threw it, and commenced tying.

"All of a sudden my hands wouldn't work," Clyde said with a tear in the corner of his eye. "It was like there was a band pulled tight around my chest."

That was the last time Clyde roped in competition.

"After that, things got worse," Clyde said. "It wasn't many years before I landed in this wheelchair." He'd been in that wheelchair for nearly thirty years. Doctors later diagnosed it as multiple sclerosis. "The world's passed me by since I got in this chair."

Clyde's wife suddenly appeared in the room. Her eyes were moist. It was obvious she'd been listening from the next room. "You should know," she said, "he's never lost hope. And you should know that in all these years I've never once heard him pout. Never heard him complain. Never heard him say a foul thing about anybody or anything."

I believed her. And I was amazed that she could honestly say it—this woman who had spent better than thirty years hand-feeding her husband, pushing him to and fro, taking him to the bathroom, dressing, bathing, grooming, understanding, and loving him.

"Only thing I regret," Clyde piped up, "is I never got to rope in that Sun Bowl."

"But he's there every year," Juanita said. "Sitting up on the top row in his wheelchair. He never misses a performance."

"I love that Dixie Roundup," Clyde said. "Those boys can rope nowadays. They make us old-timers look silly."

I smiled and nodded. "Glad I never had to rope against you," I said.

"You'd have roped circles around me," Clyde said.

It was difficult to leave, like leaving the glowing heat of a fire on a cold winter morning. Getting up to go, I shook Clyde's hand again and spent another moment lost in the flood of his blue eyes. As Dad and I walked out the front door, Clyde spoke again. We poked our heads back in to listen.

"That Tom Ferguson can rope, "Clyde said. "He'll get two tied in the time I roped one. You watch him."

"I will," I said. But walking down the sidewalk to the car, I concluded that no matter how many world titles Tom Ferguson won, Clyde McQuaid would always be my champion.

Clyde McQuaid watched his last Dixie Roundup from the seat of his wheelchair in September of 1985. He passed away at the age of seventy-four on June 25, 1986.

. . . THERE'S A FAT rattler coiled and cocked smack in the middle of the trail. Afton, he don't even hesitate. He swings down and hands the bridle reins to William.

"What are you planning to do?" William asks.

"I plan on clearing the trail," says Afton. He picks up a stick and trims it with his knife, leaving a two-pronged fork at the end of the pole. He warily approaches the dusty diamondback, muttering untoward phrases beneath his breath.

"Don't bother him!" comes back William. "He'll leave soon enough."

"This ol' boy's headed straight to the grave," utters Afton.

"You're going to kill him?"

"I sure as hellfire ain't gonna dance with him." Afton mimics a little dance on the toes of his boots as he draws close to the snake. "Sure as you're butt's sore, I'm gonna kill him."

"You can't kill him—you don't have the right."

"On the contrary," Afton says. "I've got the duty."

"This is his territory. He's part of the ecology."

"So am I," says Afton, copying William's self-righteous tone. "Do you think that somebitchin' snake'd think twice about laying his fangs in ol' Nunya's hock? I lost one of my best mounts to a rattlesnake bite. This'll make one less devil to contend with." Afton eases the stick toward the rattler's head. Suddenly an unholy buzz peppers the air.

"Hate that sound," mumbles Afton as he clamps the stick down, forking the rattler's head in the dirt. "That there sound is hard on this triple-by-pass heart of mine. Sound of death is what it is."

"Don't you kill that snake!"

"Don't you try to stop me."

That diamond-shaped head is all mouth now, wide open, gaping, fangs hanging out like horns. The thick curl of serpent wiggles and writhes as Afton pulls the knife from his pocket with his free hand, flips it open, and lays the gleaming blade clean through the neck. . . .

13   The Roundup

RODEO IS THE sport of cowboys. As if the range itself did not provide enough recreation. What it really is, is a chance to share actual ability in an artificial exhibition. Yet nowadays, the artificial act of rodeo has become actual. Top bull riders like Bobby Delvechio and Charlie Sampson come from the Bronx and from Watts, respectively. Direct from urban-street boyhoods, neither one ever spent a season on a ranch before he became a rodeo star. And many of the weekend jackpot ropers you'll see pulling shiny fifth-wheel trailers with brand new extended-cab Jimmy pickups (fifteen thousand dollars worth of horseflesh and tooled leather in that forty-thousand-dollar rig), have never thrown a loop on the open range.

Only a portion of your top rodeo performers are still ranch bred. It's a select few that learned to castrate a calf or doctor for pinkeye or break a colt before they went on the road as a modern Wild West act. It was the old kind of cowboy that used to come to the Roundup every year. Guys like Walter Shelley, Roy Kurt, Reed Mathis, and Gray Wilkin.

Walter Shelley, born 1908; died 1993. Dixie Roundup, 1935: First Place Team Roping (partner: Jack Beach), Second Place Calf Roping, Third Place Bronc Riding. Occupation: Cowhand and Jack of all Trades.

Me and my brothers, Sherman and Ray, and my cousin, Josh Welsh, drove wild horses sixty miles in off the Arizona Strip to buck in those early shows. We had an old black saddle horse we called Traveler. We'd ride him out there to gather horses, then bring him in and buck 'im with the rest of 'em. When you put a flank strap on old Traveler he'd come apart. He'd screech and draw good attention, and I won some money on him. After the rodeo we'd take the horses to Hy Prisbrey in Washington and sell them for five bucks a head.

In those days we rode broncs bareback with a rope and two hands. All we knew how to do was play on those animals, show off, so to speak, make people laugh. At one rodeo I shaved off half my beard and took care so that no one noticed. I rode this old cow, and after I got off, the old gal came running by me and knocked me over. Then I got up and showed everybody what a close shave she give me.

I came onto the Strip in 1921 when I was thirteen years old. Our family homesteaded at the head of Main Street out there. We chased a lot of horses in those days. Me and my brothers roped many a horse out in the Clay Hole country from the seat of a stripped down Ford.

I was afraid of bucking horses until I was twenty-two years old. I wanted no part of one. Then one day when we were headed to Bundyville for a dance, the old roan mare I was riding started to buck. That was when I discovered I liked it. From then on I just got wilder and wilder.

Roy Kurt, born 1912. Dixie Roundup, 1935: Second Place Bronc Riding. Occupation: Heavy Equipment Operator and Part-time Cowhand.

I was born in California and my mother died when I was young. As a kid I was in and out of orphan homes, but I spent as much time as I could at the picture show. I watched every Western I could get a dime for. That was my dream—to be a cowboy.

In 1925, I came to Central, Utah, and lived on the Hunt Ranch. By 1933, I was hooked up with Bob Hurley, Dee Burgess, and Jim Leavitt. They had pulled a string of bucking horses together and they were putting on rodeos all around the territory. They put on the forerunners to the Dixie Roundup in '33 and '34 at the old grandstands and race track where the Sun Bowl is now. For years I got on most any bronc for two dollars and fifty cents. One year I rode an old bronc they called the Chauncey Macfarlane horse. He was a giant brown work horse that threw most everybody in town off. He came out of the chute and ran like a scar't coyote halfway across the square. I reached up with my spurs and tried to get a buck out of him, then he fired while I was off balance and I went airborne.

Me and my partners took our horse string all over the country. We drove 'em cross-country wherever we went, and in the summer time it got awful hot moving horses from Enterprise to Hurricane to Cedar City. There was times when I rode seven or eight bucking horses in one day at a rodeo.

Those early days of the Roundup were a lot of fun. You'd go down to Dick's Cafe and visit with the cowboys that came to town for two or three days before the rodeo. Nowadays, the pros fly in, get on their draw, ride 'im, and then they're gone to another one.

In 1935, I had a horse roll over on me while I was punching cows near Central. Cracked my skull in four or five places and I was out for nine days. I rode more broncs after that accident than I did before, but my balance never was quite as good.

Reed Mathis, born 1907. Dixie Roundup, 1938: Third Place Calf Roping. Third Place Team Roping (Partner: Ted Yarbough.) Occupation: Rancher.

I started roping wild cattle on the Arizona Strip when I was thirteen years old. In those days you had to rope fast, 'cause when you came up on a bunch of unmarked yearlings, everybody was going after them.

Sam Radliff was my roping teacher. He came onto the Strip with Bill Shanley and he was a true hand. He was my tutor. He was also the one who entered me in my first rodeo. That was in 1929, and I didn't even know about it. I got to the rodeo which was held on the old square just below the Tabernacle, and Sam told me I was entered. So I roped. All that practice roping those mavericks out on the Strip paid off. I won first place in the calf roping. Surprised me more than it did anyone else.

Gray Wilkin, born 1922. Dixie Roundup 1946: First Place Bull Riding, First Place Bulldogging, First Place Bronc Riding, All Around Cowboy. Occupation: Saddle Maker.

I rode and roped in the Roundup for more than 30 years. I was only thirteen the year of the first official Roundup, but I rode a lot of calves and steers before that. When I was ten or eleven, Burton Burgess and me and a bunch of other kids would ride yearlings in the rodeos. You'd pay fifty cents to ride one, then they gave you a buck-fifty if you made a qualified ride, or you'd get your fifty cents back if you got bucked off.

I remember the first rodeo under the lights. It was in 1941. Paul Hill and Andy Jauregui put it on. I was home on furlough from the Army when I rodeoed that year. I missed the next four Roundups during the War, but I came back in '46 and that was my best year. I'd been in a quartermaster pack troop, a mule outfit, for the last few years of the War and I rode mules every day. When I got home, I was in shape and ready to rodeo.

In '46 I was the only rider at the Roundup with an Association Saddle. The rodeo committee rented it from me for everyone to use. In the bareback riding I drew an old mule out of Slats Jacob's string. Thing is, I just about had him rode until he stopped, turned his head back, and proceeded to take a bite out of my boot. I reached down to try and help myself and they disqualified me for touching with the free hand. But I still won the All Around.

The next guy to draw that mule wired the animal's mouth shut. The cowboy didn't get bit like I did, but as soon as the chute gate opened, that mule threw him out of the arena.

1986

CHARLIE SAMPSON RODE a bull at the Roundup in September. His plane landed at the municipal airport at 8:45 P.M. I saw him hustle down the runway behind the chutes just as they were loading the bulls. He signed a dozen autographs before he got on. The announcer sounded like a ringmaster as he set the stage for this confrontation between one of the world's best bull riders and one of the toughest bulls on the planet. Charlie made a beautiful ride, charging into the spin with his chest and free arm on every circle, flailing wide and grabbing with his outside spur, coming down on his feet after the whistle and trotting cleanly away from the storm. He tossed his hat and held his fists triumphantly in the air. The crowd went crazy. Charlie loaded his gear in his bag and hurried down the runway behind the chutes. He had a good bull drawn at Pendleton the next morning.

I looked back at Walter Shelley sitting a few seats behind me with a blanket wrapped around his feeble knees. He grinned at me and winked an eye.

. . . AFTON RUNS THE
*blade across his pants. That dark blood clings to his Wranglers like paste.
"Snake's got a lotta spirit—hard to kill," he says.*

*Sure enough, that dull brown creature still wiggles in the dirt, coiling
and uncoiling, headless as the proverbial horseman. Afton presses his boot
down on the spinning coil, all of this to the utter disgust of William who
sits steaming atop Nothin' with Nunya's bridle reins locked in his fist. Afton
bends down and grabs the quivering tail. "Got a grandson who's gonna be
tickled to get these rattles," he says. He slices off the rack of rattles with one
easy stroke and pokes it in his pocket.*

*"I can't believe you'd massacre that creature in cold blood, without prov-
ocation, without any reason whatsoever," says William.*

Afton looks up at William, disdain boiling in his eyes.

*"Listen to me, city boy, and listen good. Don't you come out here telling
me how to operate—not when you don't know the first damned thing you're
talking about. This here's my livelihood. You sit in your ivory tower back
there in town and think you've got things figured out. Well, this is where I
go to work every day. My daddy taught me never to leave a rattler alive. To
do so would be to shirk my duty. So you worry about your job, and I'll do
mine." . . .*

14   He Covered the Country

ON A STICKY summer morning we started a herd of eighty cows with calves up through the meadows of Clover Valley toward the Beaver Dam Seedplot. The sun was heavy and the air was full of moisture and my shirt clung to me like a damp rag to porcelain. The cattle crashed through the rabbit brush and flies lifted off them in legions. It was good to finally top out of the valley and start busting through the dry blackbrush. Now, instead of breathing the pungent valley air, I sifted the dry, dusty air of the hillside through my teeth.

I took the middle and Dad swung wide to one wing. A slender and handsome old cowboy popped up wherever he was needed. His name was Andy Lytle. He moved cattle by radar; there seemed to be a tracking system programed into him with a database that must have been compiled from many thousands of days in the saddle and countless individual encounters with cattle. Andy and his yellow gelding appeared wherever a cow strayed. They seemed to know what the cow was going to do before she did. In awe I watched the two of them work. They were one, actually—horse and rider melded into one efficient machine.

The other day I went to Andy Lytle's funeral. Eloquent tributes were delivered in honor of this man who had spent his life horseback. He had managed to raise a fine family and had built a reputation as an honest businessman, a civic leader, and a gentleman. At the funeral I learned for the first time that Andy had been born prematurely, with a birth weight of three pounds. His mother had wrapped him in cotton, lain him in a shoebox, and kept him warm in the oven. As she worked in the garden, Andy's mother had stuck him in a bucket and hung it from the clothesline. He was easy to keep track of until he grew old enough to straddle a horse. Then it was impossible. And it was on the back of a horse where he pretty much spent the rest of his life.

When he was a youngster, all the race horse men of southern Utah had clamored for Andy to ride their mounts. He had a gift, and he had his pick of horses and usually rode the winner. His ability with horses became legendary. He handled them with grace and a soft hand, for he was not a big man.

I listened to all of these tributes with a keen ear. I had my own memories of Andy, and they meshed perfectly with the funeral eulogies. There was the night at the ranch house in Clover Valley when he entertained us until after midnight with stories skillfully shared. He had the resonant voice of a young man, a slight pitch higher than most older men, and he talked through a smile which enlivened his words. But my most vivid memory carried me back to that day we pushed the cows onto the seedplot.

Over the edge of the valley we came upon an open flat. We were all sweat soaked now and the task was growing tedious. Andy must have sensed my boredom. He appeared beside me like a phantom and smiled. Untying his rope he said, "I see a long-eared calf up there." His expression turned impish, like that of a kid who had just thought of a prank. As he began to swing his rope he lifted his chin toward the calf and said, "You take the first shot."

I looked over at Dad who nodded his approval. Building a loop, I kicked old Judge up and trotted into the herd. Soon I realized that there were several long-ears in the bunch, so I took my pick. I zeroed in on a coal black calf whose ears flopped like pigtails at the side of his head. Judge picked him up, too, and zipped me in for a shot. The first loop hooked on a clump of blackbrush and the calf spurted off like a jet. After several tries and misses I retreated to the rear where Dad and Andy had been patiently riding and watching.

Andy smiled at me. "Don't give up," he said.

"I might as well try roping the wind," I said.

Andy looked at me again with a serious expression on his face. "Let me show you how it's done," he said. He nudged his yellow horse in the ribs and slipped smoothly into the herd. His rope, which appeared to be an extension of his arm, turned in slow motion. His movements were easy and fluid, with most of the action in his wrist. Andy let go the loop and it settled perfectly around a little long-ear's neck and he gently gathered the slack and dallied. I handed my reins to Dad and hopped off. The calf danced wildly at the end of the rope, bawling in pitiful spurts. Working my way down the rope I blocked him with my knee, grabbed his flank, and flipped him to the ground. Once Andy saw I had control, he hopped off and pulled out his pocket knife. Within a few seconds he had split the right ear and cropped the left, moving with the deft strokes of a surgeon. I took it all in as an awestruck spectator. How did he know it was Dad's calf? How did he remember Dad's mark? How could he do it all so fast, seemingly without thinking? From that moment until the day I sat on the hard church bench at his funeral, I thought of Andy Lytle as the most smooth cowboy I had ever known.

Another lingering image of that hot summer morning was how Andy had enjoyed it all. After we finished the first calf, it was as if a competition had started. There were at least two-dozen unmarked calves in the herd—some of them Dad's, some of them Andy's. Without saying anything, Andy had begun a game, the object of which was to see who could get the most roped and marked before we reached the seedplot. Dad roped his share and I finally caught a couple myself. But Andy showed us both up. Not in any haughty or boastful way, but out of sheer enjoyment. Because he was a cowboy's cowboy—just like his father had been.

When we finally reached the seedplot and pushed the cattle through the gate, we all three sat down under a juniper worn bare of its lower limbs by countless seasons of passing cattle. We pulled sandwiches and canned pop from our saddle bags and talked in the shade. That is when Andy told us the story of his father, George.

1920's

THROUGH THE SOUTH hills comes a horseman. He is slight of frame, with dancing brown eyes. He sits his tall horse well. Dropping off a ridge he rides into a shimmering green valley called Mountain Meadows. Two young girls dash out the door of a handsome frame house and run to their father who has been away many days. He sees them coming. His dark eyes sparkle. Riding closer he begins to holler: "Lutie, I say, Lutie, get me a fresh horse. And Laura, Laura, I say, pack me a lunch."

"Papa!" one of the girls cries, "Where have you been?"

"Pipe Spring," the man spritely replies.

"And Papa," the other girl cries, "where are you going?"

"Clover Valley, my dear!"

George Lytle might have spent an hour, maybe two, changing horses, stocking up provisions, and reacquainting himself with the family. Then he was off—Pipe Spring ninety miles behind him and Clover Valley another thirty before him.

That's the way the legend goes—a legend which is more likely understated than exaggerated. From the time George Hubbard Lytle started cowboying for his Uncle James Andrus on the Arizona Strip in the mid-1880s, right up to the day he died in St. George, Utah, in 1948, he rarely stopped for anything. The man arose before daylight each morning of his life and went busily about his task of making a living with livestock.

You've heard it before, the story of the American Original. He started with nothing, worked for his clothes and board, learned a trade, built himself a little empire. He became possibly the widest ranging cattleman ever to ride these parts, punching cows from the southern reaches of Mt. Trumble on the Arizona Strip, to the eastern ranges of Pipe Spring and Johnson Valley beyond Kanab, to Mountain Meadows north of St. George, and as far west as Clover Valley, Nevada, and the Tule Desert. He was a stockman, landowner, husband, father, missionary, banker, county commissioner; but first and most, he was a cowboy.

George Lytle, like many other cattlemen of his generation, was not born to be a cowboy. His father, John Milton Lytle, had come to St. George with the original Mormon pioneers in 1861. He was a horticulturist, more specifically a wine maker, and was not a stockman in any sense of the word. Young George was awakened to the lure of the range and fine horseflesh as he sat on his great-grandfather Israel Ivins' fence and admired the well-bred horses that Israel and Anthony Ivins raised.

George's uncle, James Andrus, ran the LDS Church herd for the Caanan Stock Company on the Arizona Strip and that was where George became a cowboy. The boy's formal education had been so meager he never remembered what grade he finished, but, as his son Andy remembered, he was an excellent speller and a whiz with figures. The family still possesses a book entitled *Harpers Graded Arithmetics— Second Book in Arithmetic*, copyright 1882. On the flyleaf appear the words: "This book is where I got my education by the fire light out on the cattle range at Scutampaw, Utah." Signed: "Geo. H. Lytle."

"He was a determined man," remembered Andy. "When he decided to do something, it got done. Like the time he decided he was going to catch a wild mule, and it took him two days and three horses to do it."

Chasing wild horses became a passion for George Lytle, yet it seems he did it more for the economic sense it made than for the recreation. "Father always told me not to chase horses unless I saw one I really wanted," recalled Andy. "Seems like we were both always seeing one we really wanted."

George had accumulated a fair herd of cattle by the time he left on a mission for the Mormon Church in 1897. He preached the Latter-day Saint gospel in Kentucky and Tennessee as intensely as he punched cows, and when he returned home in 1898, he went right back to the Strip and continued building his herd.

One method he used to amass his assets was to chase wild horses and bring twenty or thirty head to town at a time. He'd trade the horses to folks around town for calves. Gradually his herd increased. "When the cows saw Dad coming to town with a herd of horses, they'd start bawl-ing," chuckled Andy. "They knew he was coming for their calves."

At twenty-nine, the dark-eyed bachelor was the most eligible man in the territory. Andy said, "Mother once told me he could charm the birds right out of the trees." One day he finally discovered the petite blue-eyed blonde who had grown up across the street. Rachel Lucinda (Lutie) Pace had always been much younger, seven years younger than George, but now, suddenly, she was grown up and exciting and beauti-ful. When they married in the winter of 1900, they started out on much more than the proverbial shoestring.

Though a devoted husband and father, George Lytle was on the range much of his married life, covering every broken inch of it on horseback.

"He always went to bed with a pocket watch and a box of matches lying next to him," said Andy. "Along about three or four in the morn-ing he'd strike a match, look at his watch, and hop up. Then he'd rustle everybody else up and get a day's work done before breakfast." Later, when Andy was married himself, and his family lived in Central, he and his wife had to get up awfully early if they wanted to have breakfast ready by the time George showed up on his horse from Mountain Meadows, six miles away. "He always said a couple of hours in the morning was worth three in the afternoon," Andy remembered. "But at four in the afternoon he'd still be going as hard."

In the Lytle family you got up at 4:00 A.M., hauled hay, ate break-fast, and worked cows until lunch, then trained colts, ran races, and generally enjoyed the afternoon. "We had a lot more fun in those days than kids do now," said Andy.

Breakfast on the range, as Andy remembered it, consisted of bacon and biscuits that George made. They'd dip the biscuits in bacon grease and sprinkle sugar on them.

Around 1919, George Lytle sold his holdings on the Arizona Strip to John Findlay and John Kenney. He wanted his family closer to town, and he was disenchanted by what he called the godless Texans who were coming onto the Strip. By now he had nine children, seven of whom were living, and one more daughter soon to come. He bought the Mountain Meadows ranch, about 30 miles north of St. George, from H. J. Burgess. This verdant valley, peaceful and serene by then, had been the site of one of the darkest tragedies in Mormon history. In September of 1857, on the very land that George now owned, about 120 (the exact number is not known) wagon train emigrants had been killed as a result of complex circumstances between Mormons, Indians, and the travelers. John D. Lee, the only man tried as a result of the incident, was later executed at the site. Though some locals considered the place haunted, all of this was of no consequence to George, who envisioned the valley as the perfect headquarters for his ranching operations. The family began spending summers at Mountain Meadows and winters in St. George where the kids could attend school. Soon he purchased ranches at Pipe Spring, Arizona, and Clover Valley, Nevada. He also obtained a vast tract of winter range on the Tule Desert, north of Bunkerville, Nevada.

At the same time, George was securing a great deal of real estate around St. George. He owned several city blocks which are now part of St. George's valuable downtown district. "Dad always said, if you invest in real estate, you'll always be even with the world," Andy remembered. Yet the family sold most of those holdings long before they became the million-dollar properties they are today.

George had precious little time to spend on his business in town. With cattle in every direction of St. George, he spent weeks at a time in the saddle, riding a good horse everywhere he went. People who knew him remember him for his uncanny ability to get the best out of a horse. "He always liked a good horse," said Andy. "But he had a knack for making even a bad horse look pretty good." George Lytle's horses were always travelers, good walkers, yet the ever-rushed George was known to go at a trot most of the time.

The man's love for quality horse flesh was ultimately illustrated when he bought and imported to St. George a royal-blooded thoroughbred stallion that had run in the Kentucky Derby. Such a purchase, here on the fringes of the Great Basin, was revolutionary at the time. They called the big stud Shine, and his colts were well known for many years around this part of the country.

"You see," Andy said, "Dad got a kick out of life. He worked awful hard, but he knew how to enjoy himself. He loved to race horses and he liked to rope." The cowboys who rode with George Lytle said he could rope anything. He rode an ancient saddle with a center-fire cinch and a big metal horn. Because he was on the range so much, it was mostly other cowboys who witnessed his skills. He roped in few public rodeos.

"He roped everything by the hind hooves," said Andy. "He'd spoil you because he made things so easy. If he didn't bring a calf to the fire by two hind feet, it was because the critter had kicked one out getting there."

Andy remembered his father, at the age of seventy-six, roping and tying a bull. "That was just two years before he died and he really wasn't feeling well at the time. But he dang sure enjoyed every minute of it."

George Lytle could ride a horse further and get more out of him than most anyone. "Let's take a lantern instead of a bedroll," he often told Andy. If there was ever a moment to rest, George found something to do while he relaxed.

"One thing I respected about Dad," recalled Andy, "is he was always good to his horses. He had enough animals trained and ready that he could ride two or three different mounts a day. He was one with a horse. He could even talk one out of bucking. But he expected a lot of a horse, too." Andy recalled being out at Bunker Peak with his father and several other cowboys gathering cattle. It was midafternoon and George had a county commission meeting in town that night. He left late in the afternoon and rode his horse thirty miles to town, attended the meeting, and was back at Bunker Peak early the next afternoon.

A goer and a doer, George Lytle also had the ability to infect others with ambition. "He could get you moving," said Andy, recalling those 4:00 A.M. wake-up calls. "He worked hard and people around him worked hard—he had a way of popping those black eyes and putting the freshness back into you."

There was always a bed and something to eat for anybody passing by the Lytle Ranch. And they were many, since Mountain Meadows was smack on the main route, a midway point between a dozen destinations. "You could count on him for most anything," Andy added. "He worried about other people's cattle as much as his own. When stray cows came onto the place, he'd take care of them like they were his own until he could deliver them back or someone showed up for them."

Dignified and a lover of music, George always sang to his children and grandchildren. "He wasn't much of a singer himself, but he appreciated music," said Andy. "He liked to talk about his days out on the Strip when Bert Price would call up on the single telephone line that stretched across that remote country and sing to all the cowboys huddled around their receivers."

By the time George Lytle passed away in 1948, he had earned the recognition and respect of cowboys, businessmen, government officials, and common folk across the territory. Most everyone who knew him held a certain admiration for the man, which is quite understandable. He was a cowboy's cowboy.

. . . AFTON KICKS A hole six inches deep in the trail. He pushes the limp remains of a rattlesnake into the hole, then smooths it over with dirt. Grabbing the reins from William, he swings into the saddle and nudges Nunya with the heel of his boots. Nunya hops across the grave and trots down the trail.

Now William settles back into the saddle and gives Nothin' a flip of the reins. Nothin' won't move. The old gelding isn't about to cross that snake's grave. William grinds his heels into Nothin's ribs. "Gitty up!"

Nothing.

Afton stops, turns, watches.

Nothin' finally noses up to the spot where the snake lies beneath the surface. Suddenly the ground begins to move. Dirt spins. Nothin' snorts. The thick, humping back of a headless rattleless snake winds up out of the dirt. Its bloody tail suddenly flips free and the entire snake turns out of the ground like an auger. Nothin' rares, whirls, and, as if possessed by a demon, hightails it up the trail toward home.

Runaway! . . .

15   Of Miscues and Men

IT WAS STILL dark that October morning as we loaded the horses in the truck and headed west toward the Beaver Dam Wash. At daybreak we dropped off the slope into the sandy canyon of the wash and drove along the edge of Herb Fletcher's field, just above Motaqua. The dust in the air ahead suggested we were not the first hunters on the road that morning.

Out in the middle of Herb's field of dry grass lay a horse. I figured the animal was just resting, though it is not common to see a horse flat on his side, straight-legged, in the middle of a field at daybreak.

"What do you think?" asked Marv Jones, the big man who sat next to the passenger window with his rifle between his knees.

"I'd say he's just resting," Dad answered as he drove on toward our destination at Dodge Wash on the other side of the Beaver Dam. "There—you see?—he switched his tail."

I watched the horse closely as we drove by and in the last glimpse saw him kick a leg. It seemed an unnatural movement to me.

We unloaded at the water tanks in Dodge Wash, tied our gear to the backs of our saddles, mounted, and rode east toward the ledges above the Beaver Dam Wash. In this same draw a few weeks earlier I had helped Dad and Fenton Bowler rope a high-horned hereford cow. She was wild as a lizard. We range-loaded her in the truck, a feat I had never seen accomplished before and may never again. Loading a wild cow into a cattle truck on the open range without the aid of a corral and loading chute is something akin to herding a trout into a net with a two-inch opening. But Fenton and Dad had done it before. Employing a complex system of ropes and dallies and angles and expletives, we loaded that feral cow and hauled her straight to the packing yards.

The morning sun glittered in our faces as we pushed through the blackbrush and broke over the top where the first draw spread out like a giant V. Squinting against the sun, I looked eastward across the massive expanse of the canyon we had just crossed in the truck. I could see the long, yellow field now. It stretched away across a flat above the other side of the wash. Focusing my eyes on the field I tried to telephoto in on the horse, but it was too distant. I pulled my rifle from the scabbard and sighted through the scope. Still I couldn't see anything so small as a horse. I replaced the rifle in its leather carrier.

A skittering bunch of deer fanned out of the draw below us. I drew my .270 from the scabbard again, this time as I dismounted in a smooth motion, just the way Dad had taught me. My heart rate doubled as all the deer stopped on the broad face of a ledge, not more than a hundred yards away. I tied my horse to a bush and took a quick seat among the rocks.

The deer watched curiously as I studied them in my scope. I couldn't put antlers on any of them, though I desperately wanted to see a rack on the lead doe. She stood as broad and handsome as any buck I'd ever seen, and I wanted so badly for her to have antlers that I could almost see them. I hadn't brought a buck home in a couple of seasons, which somehow in my own way of thinking made me less of a man. Why couldn't this one be a buck? If only she were, I'd have him with one squeeze of the trigger.

"Never shoot until you're sure," Dad had always told me. From the time I was eight I'd tagged along as he chased deer from the white aspen groves atop Cedar Mountain to the thick dry oak patches of the Beaver Dam Slope. I'd watched him raise his rifle a thousand times, then lower it with restraint. Once a shell is fired, he always said, there's no calling it back. The decision is made in a split second, but that decision's components—experience, patience, horse sense—are compiled over years. Wanting it to be a buck will never make it a buck.

We jumped deer all day long. My heart got plenty of exercise. But none of the deer had antlers, and we rode back to the truck that afternoon lacking any game. It didn't bother Dad or Marv. They had nothing to prove to anyone. But there were young boys waiting at home for me, boys hoping for a big buck to hang and skin in the garage. I hated to disappoint them.

In the haze of evening we drove home, down across the wash and up the other side along Herb Fletcher's field. My heart started pounding hard as we approached the spot where we had seen the horse lying that morning. Drawing nearer now I grew short of breath. There was still a brown spot out in the field. I went numb as the sure detail of a dead horse came into sharp focus. Passing now, moving ever so slowly up the road, we all three sat silent and looked at the horse where it lay—in the very spot and in the very position as we had seen it that morning.

∪ ∃⊮ ∪

*... EARS PINNED BACK.
Tail flying. Nothin' streaks up the trail with the fear of Satan screaming
through his veins. William clings to the saddle horn, hair pasted back like
wheat in a tornado. Through the oak brush they plow, branches beating
legs. The reins are long forgotten. They lay across the mane, fully unat-
tended. William, he's sold out. Lost all reason. Right now he's in pure panic
mode.*

*Afton revs Nunya up for the rescue. He's got fifty yards to make up,
which he accomplishes in about ten seconds flat. Now he's on Nothin's tail.
"Grab the reins!" he yells.*

No response from William.

"Grab the damned reins!"

*Now it's apparent to Afton that he's dealing with a zombie. He kicks in
Nunya's afterburner and shoots up alongside Nothin'. Trees whiz by in a
blur. William's eyes are locked dead ahead. He's frozen to the horse like a
statue. Afton reaches over and gathers up the reins, pulls back with a ven-
geance, and hollers, "Whoa, you somebitch! Whoa!"*

*They stumble to a stop in a ball of dust. Afton's face is red with fury, and
William, he's white as a powdery cloud. Afton throws the reins at William's
chest. "Take 'em," he says.*

William's beside himself. Says he doesn't know what came over him.

*Then there's one of those pauses. Two grown men sittin' side by side on
the edge of Burnt Canyon and can't come up with a miserable thing to say
to each other. They might just sit there dumfounded the rest of the day if
that long-eared brindle bull doesn't pop out of the brush in front of 'em.*

*"That's him!" Afton hollers. He assumes immediate pursuit. In that one
wild moment something mighty powerful comes over William. He scoops up
the reins. He's renewed, repentant, ready to assume control of his life again.
He takes hold of Nothin' with authority, rattles the old gelding's ribs with the
heels of his hiking boots, and lays in behind Afton at a hard gallop. About
the time Afton begins to build his loop, a wicked looking zig-zag of lightning
pummels the ridge above. Its crack of thunder nearly fractures the earth. ...*

121

16   Desert Tortoise 101

MY FATHER KNOWS his turtles. The subject has become one of those necessary continuing education courses crucial to the survival of his business. He knows his turtles the way a CPA knows his new tax laws. Lately it has come down to a battle of turf between Dad's cows and the threatened desert tortoise.

1979

DAD SAT WITH a dozen of his fellow cowmen in the back of a conference room at the brand new Hilton Inn while a bearded man in a plaid flannel shirt stood at the front of the room next to a carousel slide projector and extolled the sad condition of *Gopherus agassizii*.

The desert tortoise is endangered, the man explained. Studies along the Beaver Dam Slope indicate its steady disappearance. The man, in his expressionless, scientific drone, attempted to explain why he thought tortoise numbers were declining. In essence he was saying that it was due in large part to tortoise-tromping, grazing, grass-greedy cattle. He claimed these cattle, whose owners all sat stoically in the back of the room, deprived the tortoise of feed, destroyed the tortoises' burrows, and, in general, out-competed this ancient, slow-moving, defenseless reptile.

I was sitting next to Dad. It wasn't long before he began to squirm in his seat. He was out of his habitat here in this plush carpeted room with dangling chandeliers and tinfoil wallpaper—as clearly out of his habitat as a desert tortoise in a cardboard box in some kid's backyard. Dad listened intently to the speaker, offering him the same concentrated attention he would offer anyone who addressed him. But he grew more and more impatient as the man continued his discourse.

My father was empty-handed that night. He was not armed with a briefcase full of data to refute the man in the flannel shirt who had flown in from San Francisco to enlighten him on the desert ecosystem. All Dad carried with him was a head-full of experience, a head of quickly graying hair beneath a silver-belly Stetson. He hunched forward on his chair and wrapped his crooked fingers around his knees. He could not help but squirm. The bearded man at the front of the room was now, in effect, challenging his right to graze cattle on the Beaver Dam Slope, questioning his claim to the range where his cattle wintered.

The man began to flash slides on a silky white screen. Soon he came to a photo which he claimed illustrated the destructive effects of cattle near watering holes. Dad's kind, easy eyes suddenly widened to a glare. On the screen before him flashed a picture of a small plot of desert torn apart as if by a bulldozer. Dad knew the location. It was near his allotment. It was a cleared spot just off a dirt road, a place that had been 'dozed during construction of a cattle guard.

He shot to his feet and blurted, "If this is the kind of flimsy evidence you're basing all of this on, we ain't none of us got a chance."

From there the proceedings deteriorated. The cattlemen had entered the meeting like stunned tigers thrown into a cage. It took them a while to adapt to the garish surroundings, to adjust their outdoor eyes to the artificial light. They began to growl and then to roar, and by the end of the night the bearded man in the flannel shirt was lucky to escape with it still on his back.

1989

THE TORTOISE–COW dilemma began to simmer that night as the 1970s dissolved into the 1980s. As the decade progressed, the dilemma worked its way into a serious confrontation, and as the '80s faded, Dad and his fellow ranchers found themselves convened at another hearing, the last showdown, this one in the Christmas decorated chambers of the St. George City Council.

The bearded man in the flannel shirt didn't show this time. His work was finished. He and his fellow petitioners had finally succeeded in gaining emergency endangered status for the desert tortoise through the U.S. Fish and Wildlife Service. The only thing standing in the way of permanent endangered status was the formality of a few public hearings and a ruling from the bureaucracy.

"It don't matter what we say tonight," Dad mumbled to the other cowmen who stood around the back of the hall before the meeting started. "It's cut and dried. The turtles are on and we're off." But Dad was determined to make his last stand. He'd march up to the mike, state his name and occupation, and go on record. He'd see to it that the official transcript contained a little horse sense. That was the problem, as far as Dad could see it: too much muck and very little clear thinking.

During the '80s Dad and all of his cattlemen colleagues had become self-taught experts on this ancient desert species known officially as *Gopherus agassizzii.* They knew, for example, that the prehistoric looking creature is the largest reptile in the arid southwestern United States, and that it historically occupies a range including a variety of desert communities in southeastern California, southern Nevada, western and southern Arizona, southwestern Utah, and on down through Sonora and northern Sinaloa, Mexico.

My father knew that tortoises spend much of their lives in underground burrows which they excavate to escape the harsh summer and winter weather of the desert. And that the tortoises usually emerge in the early spring and in the autumn to feed and mate, although they may be active during the summer when temperatures are moderate. He was also very much aware that tortoises are vegetarians, eating a variety of herbaceous vegetation, especially the flowers of annual plants. He knew that the tortoise is vulnerable to a number of threats, the highest on the list being "habitat degradation" caused by (in the order listed by the U.S. Fish and Wildlife Service) off-road vehicles, desert training maneuvers, various kinds of mining, grazing by cattle and sheep, and agricultural and residential development. Next comes "taking," which is the killing or collection of individual tortoises, then predation, by such predators as ravens and coyotes, and, finally, fragmentation of habitat resulting from any of these factors.

These, my father knew, had been the key bargaining chips for the desert tortoise protectionists all through the '80s, the tools with which they tried to build their case for endangered status. But they had so far been unsuccessful in gaining more than a "threatened" listing, and that was for the Beaver Dam Slope population only. They had tried in 1980, and again in 1984, and though the Fish and Wildlife Service had listened sympathetically, the listing had been precluded by proposals with higher priority. It would take some evidence with a little more punch to get the point across, and that evidence miraculously surfaced near the end of the decade.

It was called respiratory disease syndrome. This, as Dad would realize when he read in the Federal Register of October 13, 1989, had become the *coup de gras* for tortoise preservationists, the missing wrench needed to bolt together a solid case for endangered status. Respiratory disease syndrome was believed to be spreading in the wild population, threatening to reach epidemic proportions.

Something was spreading all right. Dad figured he could sure enough smell it spreading across the landscape in epidemic proportions—the same stuff he recycled out of his corrals into Mom's flower bed every spring.

He walked to the microphone and placed his papers on the podium. He'd left his hat back on the seat. TV cameras pointed at him like artillery, and heavy lights bore down upon him more intensely than the pounding sun over the Beaver Dam Slope. He pulled a handkerchief from his back pocket and wiped his brow and began to read from the crinkled paper in his trembling hand.

"If you are truly concerned about the condition of the desert tortoise," Dad told the government officials seated on the stand that night, "then let's spend our time and effort looking for the real culprits. The Beaver Dam Slope population of the desert tortoise was listed as threatened in 1980. That's been nearly ten years ago. New grazing systems have been implemented in favor of the tortoise, and one large area was completely fenced off from grazing. Yet you say the population is still declining, even in that excluded area where no grazing has occurred in nearly a decade. Let's be careful before we hang the blame for this on cattle."

All the cattlemen in the room that night knew where the turtles had gone. Anyone who grew up in the tri-state country surrounding the Beaver Dam Slope knew where thousands of tortoises went during the 1930s, '40s, '50s, and '60s. They disappeared from the desert and reappeared in the backyards of local children. Hundreds of kids in southwestern Utah remember having at least one of these dusty, ancient creatures penned in a cardboard box in the back yard. Desert tortoises were picked up by the score down along old U.S. 91 where it crossed the Slope on the west side of Utah Hill. You could take them to "Beaver Dam Bill" who had a shop near the Beaver Dam Lodge and he'd give you a buck for each one. That was in the days when a dollar was a dollar and you could make a fair wage just plucking turtles off the highway. In turn, "Beaver Dam Bill" sold them to tourists at a dollar or two profit.

Kids in St. George would drill a hole in the turtle's shell and hook a chain to it, then tether the chain to a rock or tree to keep their pet in check. They painted all kinds of colorful designs on turtles' backs—from American flags to checker boards. Some tortoise experts believe that as many as 100,000 tortoises have been held in captivity throughout the Southwest.

Dad finished his testimony and tried to brush off the rousing applause as he returned to his seat. He thought he had made his last stand. Now his future lay in the hands of the bureaucracy. He sat down and listened to the rest of the hearing. He heard his fellow cattlemen cite studies which refuted claims that the Beaver Dam Slope is overgrazed. He listened to arguments that cattle and turtles can coexist in harmony. He even heard one cowboy ask the Fish and Wildlife lawyer who sat on the stand whether or not the effects of downwind radiation from atomic testing at Yucca Flats had been considered.

None of the cowmen refuted the fact that tortoise numbers had declined; they simply defended their contention that cattle had not contributed to it. After all, they countered, cattle only graze the areas within five miles of water holes, and tortoise habitat covers hundreds of square miles beyond those limits. What's more, tortoise habitat covers only the winter range of cattle, which means that for the most part, the cows are there when turtles are deep in their dens, and when the turtles come out to feed, the cattle are generally gone to other pastures. Besides, they wondered, if cattle are to blame, why were tortoise numbers highest in the early part of the century when grazing was not controlled and cattle numbers were also at their peak?

"How can you take twenty-one million acres of public land out of multiple use to preserve a species, when estimates exist that as many as two million individuals of that species roam the deserts of the Southwest?" asked one cowman. "The tortoise is a surrogate," said another rancher. "You're making him a surrogate, like the spotted owl in the Northwest. You are using the endangered listing of the tortoise to remove cattle from the range. You are making a big mistake."

Dad listened to it all calmly. He had learned not to overreact. He knew the bureaucracy would do what the bureaucracy would do. It would not help if he lost his temper and vented the frustrations that steamed inside him. He would hold fast against the pressure. He would continue to produce. He would keep producing until he died, and if no one wanted to produce after that . . .

A front page story appeared in the local paper the next day. It recapped the hearing and quoted my father's testimony. The story pointed out that testimony against the endangered listing of the desert tortoise outnumbered testimony for it by more than ten to one. The hearing had been a victory, for the time being, in favor of the cattlemen.

A few days later a letter to the editor appeared on the editorial page of the local paper. "How can anyone make a desert into a grazing land?" wrote the irate reader. "Get rid of the cows. Save the turtles!"

1993

IT WAS EARLY March. I had just dropped my son and his friend off at the movies. They had been waiting for this one for a long time—*Teenage Mutant Ninja Turtles III*. They thought I was crazy because I had no desire to go with them. I told them I'd pick them up in two hours, then I drove down Flood Street to Dad's house to see how his day had gone.

Turned out it had been a banner day for Dad. One of those rare victorious days when things finally go right. He had just gotten home from Las Vegas where he had spent the day in a courtroom listening to testimony regarding whether or not a fellow rancher would have to pull his cattle off the Mormon Mesa from March through the middle of June to make way for the desert tortoise. [*Lundgren, et al.*, v. *Bureau of Land Management* (National Resources Defense Council, Sierra Club, Desert Protective Council intervenors), March 1–3, 1993, U.S. Department of the Interior, State of Nevada, Office of Hearings and Appeals Hearing, before The Honorable John Rampton, Adminstrative Law Judge.]

The rancher had received a "full force and effect" order from the Bureau of Land Management, which he had appealed. The result was a three-day hearing before an administrative law judge who had, after hearing testimony from range experts, ruled that the rancher would not have to comply with the order—at least not this year. Rather than rebut the rancher's case, the attorneys for the BLM, along with an intervening attorney for the Sierra Club, the Natural Resources Defense Council, and the Desert Protective Council, argued that the judge did not have jurisdiction, a matter which would have to be settled later. In the meantime, however, there had been a small victory in favor of a rancher. A judge had heard testimony and ruled that at least for another year a rancher could continue to coexist with the tortoise.

Dad sat relaxed on the couch and savored it all with a wide grin. "Never thought I'd see it," he said. "That judge, bless his good old heart, he had some common sense. He listened to it all and then he just told those BLMers plain and simple that there was no reason why cows and turtles can't live together on that desert. I'm telling you, there was range scientists there from all over Nevada and Utah testifying how there's no documentation to show that cows harm tortoise habitat at all. Fact is, one of them even brought up the idea that cows actually benefit the tortoise. He talked about how grazing stimulates vegetative production on the range, and how excluding grazing can cause a range to stagnate, get woody, get decadent. He used a chart that showed how tortoise numbers were at their peak in the 1920s and 30s before the Taylor Grazing Act when cattle numbers were at their highest point. Since cattle grazing has been reduced in the 1960s, '70s, and '80s, the tortoise numbers have fallen, too."

I sat there and listened intently. This was Dad's hour of glory, and I shared it with him by letting him relive the entire hearing.

"They had one witness there, a prominent history professor from up north, who brought up something I hadn't ever thought of before," said Dad. "This guy is an expert on the diaries of the early explorers of southern Utah and Nevada, and he's studied the Indian legends of the natives that were already here. He said he's read dozens and dozens of journals and diaries and letters and official reports that people wrote in the 1700s and 1800s, and said it is very, very rare, almost never, that you find them mentioning anything at all about tortoises. And yet, in the mid-1900s, that's all anybody saw when they drove down across the Slope on Highway 91. He said the Indian legends that were compiled by the early researchers contained no references to the desert tortoise, in spite of the fact that they included stories about thirty or forty different animals that were part of their lives in those days. Those Indians saw special mystical qualities in the animals that lived among them and they told and retold legends about them, and even though the rabbits and deer and hawks and coyotes were included, for some reason they didn't mention the tortoise except in one recorded story of the Southern Paiute.

"Then there were the Spanish explorers like Dominguez and Escalante, who never mentioned a tortoise, even though they tromped one step at a time through this whole country, and there was John C. Fremont, James O. Pattie, Jedediah Smith, and the pioneers who came through in their wagons, traveling in the cool part of the day, the same time tortoises would be out of their dens. All of them kept meticulous records of their trips, noted all the things they saw and experienced. But no tortoises. You'd think if the tortoise was there, if he'd been a source of food or if his shell had been used for practical purposes—as you would certainly think it would have—then there would be at least some mention of the animal in all those documents. The thing of it is, these weren't people zippin' down 91 in their Cadillacs. These were people on horseback, in wagons, walking. Took 'em a long hard day to cover twenty miles. And I'm here to tell you, if there had been turtles around, they would have seen 'em."

At this point I figured one question of cross examination wouldn't hurt. I asked Dad what he thought the historian's testimony proved.

"I'll tell you what it proves," he replied, scooting up quickly to the edge of the couch. "It proves that there weren't that many, if any, turtles out on that range a hundred or two hundred years ago. What it tells me is that turtles never became an item around here until cattle did. Hey, if those environmentalists want to grow more turtles, they ought to pray for more cows. More cows, more turtles, more power to everybody."

Dad rested his case, once and for all.

I hurried back to the cinema to pick up the kids from the movie. All the way home I thought about the things Dad had said while the boys in the back seat relived their thrilling evening at the movies. Between thoughts I picked up on snatches of conversation regarding hip turtles named after Renaissance artists. These most excellent reptiles had emerged from the sewers, taken on superhuman qualities, become fine ninja fighters, and developed a distinct taste for pizza. When I dropped my son's friend off, he thanked me as he sprang out of the car. He took off at a run for the front door, then stopped suddenly, turned in his tracks, raised his fist in the air, and yelled, "Turtle Power!"

. . . THIS LONG-EARED BRINDLE
bull's got horns half the width of Lincoln County. All the better to navigate by. Afton follows those galloping horns as if they're landmarks standing up there before him like the Grand Tetons.

Rain's coming down in sheets now. William's in the process of recovering his pride—lack of rain gear notwithstanding. Soaked to the bone, he's in the chase with gusto.

Afton floats his first loop cleanly over the brindle's horns. He jerks the slack and takes three firm dallies of the saddle horn. Ol' Nunya slows against the bull's stout pull, but fails to bring the charging brindle to a halt. Afton spies a well-anchored juniper tree up ahead. He elects to fork it, executing perfectly. The bull cuts to the right; Afton and Nunya shy to the left. Rope broadsides the solid juniper, and that bull flips around it like the tail of a whip. One revolution. Two. Now the bull is dallied to the tree. Trapped.

William pulls to a stop and watches this impressive display. He's content to spectate, but Afton needs his help. "Git down and tie this rope off," orders Afton. "I gotta put a loop on his hind legs."

"Me?" replies William with a blank look on his face.

"No," Afton grumbles. "The rat in your pocket."

William slides down slowly. His legs are hurtin' and he walks as if on coals. He makes his way carefully to the tree, eying the bull with every step.

"He ain't gonna hurt ya," Afton assures him. "He's all blow and no show. Just ease up there like you mean it and I'll let go my dally. Then you can tie it off with a half hitch."

William's hands are trembling, as any man's would under similar circumstances. The bull hangs like a lead anchor at the end of the rope, muzzle flaring, eyes bulging like shiny eight balls. Afton lets loose the rope and William nervously throws the hitch. As he pulls the tail through to finish the knot, the bull blows a storm of snot, throws his head back, and charges William like a ball out of a cannon.

William departs with the miraculous speed that only pure adrenaline provides. But not fast enough to elude the forehead at the front of fifteen-

hundred pounds of crossbred bull, which, in short order, launches William into a cartwheel, the apex of which is higher than your average juniper. . . .

17   Saving the Place

TALMAGE LYTLE NEVER got overly excited about things. He was an easy-going cowboy whose roundish face and features bore an uncanny resemblance to W. C. Fields. That resemblance was further sustained by the distinctive high pitch in Tal's voice. He was a man who enjoyed life by the day, savoring each minute as it passed. He loved his quiet little place there along the banks of the Beaver Dam Wash, appreciated it as much as anyone ever could have. He never branched into such pursuits as bird-watching or counting plants—despite the fact that he lived in a veritable Mecca for such activities. He ran a few cattle, raised some tasty fruit, and generally enjoyed three decades of quiet life on his place there at the bottom of the canyon where the Bull Valley Wash cuts into the Beaver Dam. These days he's living out his retirement in a comfortable condo in town.

Of course Tal knew there was something special about that place where beavers worked nights in the nearby stream and ducks skimmed the surface of a tiny reservoir. There had to be. Otherwise, why would all those professors, students, researchers, school children, Boy Scouts, and bird-watchers show up every spring in their funny looking short pants, with binoculars hung around their necks, and notebooks falling out of their pockets? They came to witness the many wonders of this 450-acre paradox, just 2,800 feet above sea level, where less than ten inches of rain falls a year, and groves of Fremont cottonwood trees mingle with flowering cactus, Indian paintbrush, wild marigold, and sego lilies.

To Tal, it was not so important that his ranch on the wash happened to sit in the middle of a great transitional zone at the vortex of the

Mojave Desert, the Great Basin, and the Colorado Plateau—home of numerous rare species and a rich diversity of plant, bird, and fish life found nowhere else in Utah. It was simply home, plain and comfortable and pretty; and he gave no never-mind if those academic and sight-seeing types wanted to keep coming back.

Tal was also aware of his ranch's rich history. Captain John C. Fremont had been one of the first Anglo explorers to lay eyes on the place when he camped at the mouth of the Beaver Dam Wash in 1844. It wasn't until the Mormons settled southwestern Utah that anyone gave thought to actually living on a permanent basis there in the canyon that Indians called Motaqua (a place of dark shade). But in the late 1880s, when federal marshals began tracking down Mormon polygamists, Thomas Sirls Terry, prominent Latter-day Saint leader in southern Utah, established his third wife Hannah Louisa and her five children there in exile. Hannah's sixth child, a girl, was born during that period at the ranch. The child's name became Hannah Louisa Exile, and she was known throughout her life as Exie.

Hannah developed much of the ranch with her own hands. Her first home at the wash was a wagon box. Later her husband built a log dwelling for the family. Their food came from Hannah's garden which she watered from a reservoir built with crude tools. The arduous work, particularly the time spent wading in the reservoir to patch leaks, ruined Hannah's health, and she suffered severe rheumatism the remainder of her life. She left the ranch in 1912.

John Eardley, his wife, and six children came next. In 1928, John built the adobe ranch house which stills stands. Eardley wrested a living from the ranch for many years. He cleared the fields, built a new reservoir, dug ditches, planted an orchard, and fenced the place. When Tal Lytle and his wife bought the ranch in the 1950s they became the owners of a self-contained Shangri-la thirty miles from any form of civilization.

For thirty years the Lytles had enjoyed a secluded, comfortable life on the Beaver Dam Wash. The cows wintered right there around the place, grazing up and over the edges of the canyon and across the

Joshua slopes. In the spring old Tal would hook up with all the other cowmen at the Upper Well and gather his few dozen head for the drive onto Clover Mountain. He'd sell enough calves each fall to pay most of the bills and keep gas in the truck for supply runs to town. Meantime, he and his wife Marie took care of an orchard and garden—weeding, pruning, irrigating, and picking. Nights they relaxed in the old adobe house under venerable poplar trees and listened to coyotes and crickets, and beavers at work just a hundred yards away.

Then in the spring of 1984 things changed. Marie, who had been ill for some time, passed away. Suddenly Tal was alone at the ranch. Alone in his remote corner of the world. There were visitors from time to time. Neighboring cowboys like Fenton Bowler and Dennis Iverson stopped in on their way through, and curious sight-seers still dropped in regularly. But now that his wife was gone, none of it seemed to matter any more. It was time for Tal to retire. Time to move into a condo in town and maybe learn to golf or whatever it was town people did. When he put the ranch up for sale, folks from the university came by and asked if he would consider making the place a gift to the institution. It would make an ideal field research station, they told him.

"That would be wonderful," Tal responded. "But there's something you folks don't understand," he explained. "You've all got your pensions waiting when you retire; your check will still keep coming. I'm a cowman. This is all I've got. And it's been all I could do to hold it together this long. Am I supposed to give away my retirement?"

The professors caught his drift. It had not dawned on them that a cowman, an owner of land, would be anything but wealthy.

"It ain't like in the movies," Tal said. "Business is business and this one's no bed of roses. People figure they're givin' us that grass out there. Well, we pay our fees. It ain't no dole. I was never given nothin'. And now they're bellyachin' 'cause they think we oughta pay higher fees. Well, they oughta figure it all out on paper like I have to, and then they'd see that it ain't no handout."

The professors began to look for funds to buy the ranch. They moved quickly, knowing that Tal would sell the place to the first bidder.

They could not live with the thought of this ranch remaining in private hands when so many students and researchers and nature lovers could benefit so immensely from its unique characteristics.

Enter the Nature Conservancy. The nonprofit conservation organization lent its legal and real estate expertise to the university. A joint venture was proposed and accepted. The Nature Conservancy bought the ranch from Tal, who packed up and moved to town.

"The Lytle Ranch is a unique conservation opportunity which needed immediate attention," said the university representative at the ranch's dedication as a nature preserve. "The property is extremely valuable to science and education. So many water-associated lands in southern Utah are fast being converted to ranchette-type developments. The biological heritage of the area is at stake. It seems prudent to try and preserve natural areas like this which are natural museum pieces, and exemplary of the pristine landscapes the pioneers once knew."

I visited Tal's place not long ago. It still sits bright and serene in the middle of a bleak desert, two miles from the Nevada border in the extreme southwestern corner of Utah. Lying like an emerald in the bottom of a smoothly carved gray canyon, it glimmers up a welcome as you gaze down on it from where the road drops off the ravine's edge. It is found where you would least expect it, visible from only a short radius. And it is true what they say that few regions in the Southwest possess the botanical and biological diversity of the Lytle Ranch. It is a "contact" zone between the Mojave and Great Basin habitat types. Water flows steadily here and beavers actually live on the property, building dams in the sparse, sparkling water near Tal's old house. Beavers, here in the middle of a Joshua forest.

I walked across the bottomland with two men from the university. Their sentences stumbled over one another as each strained to describe the uniqueness of this place. They talked of gray and red and kit fox, bobcats, roadrunners, lizards and rattlesnakes, Gila monsters, cougars, desert tortoise and ringtail cats, western kingbirds, vermilion flycatchers, Gamble's quail, doves, blacktail gnatcatchers, and Costa hummingbirds.

We watched a flock of orioles dive out of the blue, sunlight splashing off their yellow feathers. They came to roost in a giant fig tree where they'd been feasting for two weeks. Once the tree was clean, they would move on.

We weaved through desert willow and pulled the yellow blossoms from creosote bushes. As we walked, the professors identified plants, rattling them off like kids naming their favorite baseball players. "If we had given this corner of the state to Arizona or Nevada," the older one said, "we would have given up twenty percent of the flora and fauna species found in Utah. There are four hundred to five hundred plant species occurring here that occur nowhere else in the state." Then with a chuckle, he added, "You could pick up a rock and throw it in just about any direction and chances are it would hit a plant that doesn't exist anywhere else in the state."

The man had found several new "state records" here (plants that have never been identified in the state before). As we arrived back at the porch of Tal's old house, the senior professor pulled out a stack of newspapers and lay the stem of an exotic looking plant between two sheets. He opened an ancient looking logbook and said, "That's number 23,650."

"Here?" I asked.

"No," he chuckled. "In my career."

I asked the younger fellow how many he had. Just over 1,800. Needless to say, the younger man looked up to the older as a guru. "But I've found five new plants on the property just this summer," he added.

"We will make vital use of this property," the older man said. "And at the same time, we will preserve it for future generations to enjoy."

The younger fellow handed me an apple he had picked from one of Tal's twisted trees. "What we have here is the least disturbed riparian habitat in the Virgin River Drainage," he said. "There are twenty species of birds here found nowhere else in Utah. It's also a critical habitat for a small fish called the Virgin River Spinedace, as well as the purple hedgehog cactus. We've got tortoises, sidewinders, Gila monsters, a Joshua tree forest, and numerous raptor species. And, most enchantingly, beaver—scores of miles from any other population of beaver. But the most unbelievable thing to me is this orchard. I mean, who would expect to be driving across the desert and come upon an orchard of fig trees, pomegranates, English walnuts, apples, plums, almonds, mulberries, apricots, peaches, and pears?"

Tal Lytle wouldn't be surprised, I thought. He'd spent half his life here. But this isn't his place anymore. Professors and students and bird-watchers from every corner of the world will busily count and preserve the flora and fauna of Lytle Ranch for years to come, while Tal and his stories grow old in a condo back in town.

. . . RAIN'S FALLING BY
the barrel-ful now. William's head pops up from behind a clump of black-
brush. There's a smile clean across his face and this journalist rises to his feet
with new life.

"Well I'll be dipped," Afton bellows. "That was one hellavu tumble you
took, boy. Looked to me like I'd be leadin' you outa here strapped across ol'
Nothin's back. And there you be—resurrected and ready fer another round.
You've got a whole lot more gumption than I had you figured for."

William, he's looking a little skee-wampus, but he's in one piece, and
apparently he's not quitting. Afton rides around and slips a loop under the
long-eared bull's hind legs. He pulls it up and dallies, then backs Nunya
away until the bull is stretched full-out—tree to horns with one rope,
hooves to saddle horn with the other.

William's still scraping mud off his shirt and pants and face. Afton steps
down, leaving the rope half-hitched to the saddle horn atop Nunya. Will-
iam watches as Nunya continues to tug backward, keeping the rope good
and stiff. Bull's bellerin' now. Tryin' to out-do the thunder. Afton works his
way down the rope, putting full faith in that cedar tree and Nunya. He
pulls his knife and goes to work. Splits the right ear, crops the left.

"Are you going to brand him?" William asks. He's inched up to the hard
breathing bull now and he can see the blood spurting from the cropped left
ear.

"We'll corral 'im for the night, and I'll brand 'im in the chute tomor-
row," says Afton. "Least he's marked. He ain't a long-ear anymore. Belongs
to somebody now."

William unties the rope from the tree while Afton, back aboard Nunya,
keeps the rope tight on the bull's hind legs. Showing remarkable courage this
time, William loosens and pulls the rope from the bull's horns, bloodying
his wet, trembling hands in the process. He's placed all his faith in Afton
now, Afton and Nunya and that dripping nylon rope which is the only
thing that separates himself from another fullgainer through the forest.
Once William is mounted, Afton backs his horse around, pivoting the bull

in the dirt until he's aimed directly up the trail. Then he turns loose the rope and the brindle shoots headlong up the country.

They follow him at a fast clip all the way up the mucky trail, two hours of teeth rattling trot, past Mud Spring, through the oak brush jungle under the pounding rain, all the way to the summit corral where the trucks are parked.

Without any instruction, William and Nothin' swing wide and head the bull through the corral gate. Afton follows the brindle in, swings the gate shut, and steps down. For a full long minute he stands there in the rain and looks down at the mud. William can't muster the strength or the courage to swing out of the saddle. His legs are wasted and he doesn't want to move. He sits atop Nothin' like a stuffed knight, rain streaming off his shoulders.

Finally Afton looks up. It ain't a pretty sight. William's nothing but a ball of mud sprinkled with red splotches of blood. It's all the old boy can do to keep from laughing.

Then the rain stops.

It's quiet for a long satisfying moment.

"You okay?" Afton asks.

William smiles. "Never been better," he says.

"Nice work," says Afton. . . .

18   Paradise Lost

1984

THEY CALL THIS place Paradise Canyon. When I was a kid we'd ride up here all the time, winding through the creosote, scraping our legs against these sandstone boulders, all the way up to that clump of green cottonwoods in the red cove to the right. Prettiest place on earth, I always thought. My friend and I played cowboys and outlaws all through these sandy washes. One of us would hole up in a chasm where flash floods had washed under a bank and let the other try to find him. Good times those were. Carefree. No concerns above spelling tests and lunch money.

This was a fine place to ride colts, leg them up and take the edge off them. It was a prime place to just ride and dream. I always figured if I ever had to run from the law, as innocent people sometimes do, I would hide away in those puffy looking rocks up on the ridge. They'd never find you there, not even in a helicopter. You'd have to take water and some jerky. With a .22 you could get yourself a rabbit every day without going far, and maybe a Gila monster once in a while.

A few months back I took some pictures of Arnold Palmer over on that ledge. The clubhouse is going on the slope just above the ridge, and you'll tee off right there where Palmer was standing. You'll stroke the ball off the cliff and it will drop some fifty vertical feet before it hits the fairway, right about here where I'm sitting on my old roan horse, Ben.

Ben doesn't know his way around this canyon the way Judge did. Judge and I spent a good part of our youth up here. We both turned twelve the same year. Over on the side of that ridge to the west, the one that looks like a long ocean liner, is where Judge cut out and left me one afternoon when I got off for personal reasons. He was waiting at the corral gate when I finally got back, pawing a hole in the dirt as if he intended to tunnel under to get home.

Arnold Palmer talked into my tape recorder and said this was one of the most beautiful locations he'd ever seen for a golf course. I said that's probably what you say about every course you design. But, no, he assured me, this one is different. And he pledged to create here one of his finest courses. His face was bronze and his hair was silver and he wasn't near as tall as I thought he would be. He had that outdoor look which I had seen in older cowboys, except his was a lotioned-down look. He didn't carry the hard marks of labor, but rather the soft evidence of sunshine. He flew in on a Lear jet with an entourage of a half-dozen. I watched the jet bank low from the north and drop to the airstrip on the black ridge above town. He'd never been here before. In a couple of quick hours he walked the eighteen proposed holes his chief architect had laid out, made a comment here and a suggestion there, then offered his approval of progress to date. An hour later he was back in his jet on a direct course for Palm Springs.

I'm not supposed to be here. Back at the entrance I had to sneak through a gate with a sign on it that said:

CONSTRUCTION AREA
DO NOT ENTER

They're going to plant this sandstone into grass and start chasing small white balls around it.

Things slip away. It makes no difference how strong your grip is.

1971

WE USED TO have a horse we called the Yellow Mare. She was a bunchy quarter horse, the traditional kind with hind quarters that didn't quit. She turned white in the wintertime, but slicked off golden every spring. I liked everything about her except a couple of nervous habits. She bopped her lips, like Mr. Ed, which is a trait that has run down through her progeny and become a kind of trademark of our herd. She also had a quick, choppy gait. Nonetheless she moved on a level plane and was surprisingly smooth to ride.

It was a perfect summer day out at Clover Valley when I was a kid. That morning I walked down the dusty lane to the Timothy Meadow where a dozen horses were pastured. The Timothy Meadow, maybe twenty acres of bright, blue green grass, sparkled in the easy morning light. Starlings and sparrows chirped low across the dewy blades. The morning air was perfectly mellow.

I gazed down the valley, following the long narrow meadows that lined each side of the railroad tracks. On the far side of the tracks lay the biggest meadow of all—the Jack Meadow, as Dad called it. Hafen Brothers had purchased it from Jack Simkins when Jack sold out and moved his family to Centerfield, Utah, where he bought a farm-ranch operation. My only memory of Jack Simkins happened on a sultry afternoon when I was nine or ten. I had been stuck on the back of a horse with vague instructions to help move an ungainly and completely stubborn herd of bolly-faced cows out of that giant green meadow. It was like trying to push ten bagfuls of marbles through the living room door with nothing but a couple of tooth-picks. When I didn't swing wide and pick up a group of rebellious wanderers, as I was expected to, Jack began to holler at me in a loud, angry voice—and I froze. I was so scared I could do nothing. Jack kept yelling and I sat stalled in my place, and when they finally got the cattle out of the meadow I was still sitting there crying and Jack rode up to me full of remorse, apologizing all over himself, and asking my forgiveness for him having lost his temper like that. I told him I was sorry and that I hadn't known what to do. He talked me through what I should have done, and I assured him that I'd do better next time.

There never was a next time. Soon after that, Jack sold all his cattle and his permit and his beautiful meadow to my dad and his brothers.

He figured he could make a better and less hectic living somewhere else. Which he did, until a few years ago when he died in a farming accident. He was killed while working under his feed truck and the hoist on the dump bed gave way.

There in the middle of the field, a hundred yards away, stood the horses. Their colors cut sharp shapes against the rich green backdrop: sorrels, bays, roans, blacks, and one yellow.

I climbed the fence, and as I hopped to the ground on the inside, the horses raised their heads one by one and began trotting toward me. They were in for a sad surprise because I carried no grain, and they would be expecting some. Not until then did I realize what a disappointment it would be for them.

The horses came at me in a swarm, jumping to a stop immediately in front of me, muzzles rooting for the bait. They nosed me a moment, checking my hands, my pockets, my feet. They hung around just long enough to confirm that I was grainless, and I could feel their disgust. Old Hector blew his nose on me and pivoted. He took off like a shot and all the others followed except one.

The Yellow Mare remained, bopping her lips and checking me over. She wasn't giving up. She'd find where I had hidden that grain. I patted her neck and apologized, rubbing a shine into that golden coat and saying silly things to her. I walked around the mare, sized her up, rubbed her some more. She bopped her lips and wouldn't leave.

Suddenly, with no forethought, I grabbed the tuft of the Yellow Mare's mane and swung onto her back. No bridle. No saddle. Just me and the mare. She stood stiff for a moment, then whirled toward the open meadow and broke as if from the starting gates. I was committed now.

Stuck.

The Yellow Mare gained speed as she raced toward the other horses now grazing peacefully on meadow grass. I clung tight to her back, my legs hooked to her girth, fingers laced snug in the mane.

The air whipped my face. Water edged out the corners of my eyes and streamed quickly back to my ears. The mare built even more speed. As we drew closer, the other horses threw their heads in the air and began to snort and squeal. A stampede commenced, a wild and random rush across the meadow—a pandemonium over which I had no control.

The end of the meadow was still a football field away. A surge of glory ran through me and I hollered from deep in my chest. The other horses ran close behind us, pounding through the soft grass, necks extended, manes flying, muzzles reaching. Now there were horses ahead, horses to the side, horses behind.

Suddenly that glorious feeling turned hollow. I was trapped. Fear spread through me now. The fence ahead grew larger and larger. I tightened my grip and hunched against what would surely be a sudden stop. For a fraction of a second I thought of selling out by swinging a leg over the withers and crashing into the grass. But this, I quickly realized, would place me smack in the path of stampeding hooves. All I could do was hang tight—take what might come.

Ten yards from the fence the Yellow Mare locked all four legs, driving them into the spongy meadow floor. Ten yards of perfect skid—two parallel lines of torn grass. My chest rammed into the mare's neck and I slid up onto her ears, then tumbled over the fence and into the brush on the other side.

The Yellow Mare and all the other horses were gone in the morning sun. I lay spread-eagle across a dusty clump of sharp smelling rabbit brush. My temples pounded. I looked down at my throbbing right hand and the locks of golden mane still woven in my fingers.

1988

LAST SPRING I helped my father gather cattle out on the Toquap range where they winter now. We rode across the western reaches of the Beaver Dam Slope, dodging the giant Joshua whose arms pointed westward toward the promised land—the Gold Coast of California where many of my father's boyhood friends had gone as young men to seek their fortunes. We wound through the creosote, sidestepped the yucca and oos and prickly pear, and clinked across the slate and shale that capped the landscape. The cows were strung ten miles wide along that vast, shimmering range. It looked as if nothing could live there but lizards, yet there had been some rain that winter and the cattle were fat and slick.

"This is new range, you know," my father said as we rode deeper into it. "There was never a cow on these sections, ever, until we opened it ten years ago."

"Why not?" I asked.

"Simple," he said. "No water." He began to hum, as he always does when he rides. I had asked a silly question. A question which exposed the fact that I, like my grandfather, had foresaken a potential life on the range for a career behind a desk. Of course I should have known the answer to my question. I knew that my father spent most of his winters hauling water. For ten winters now he had hauled that precious liquid in a giant tank strapped to a tenuous 1950s GMC. Beginning early in the morning he would fill the tank and make a run from town, some thirty-five miles one way. If more water was needed, he'd make two runs, or three. During some dry periods he might haul water twenty-four hours at a stretch—no doubt dreaming all the while of the fresh flowing well at Rock Canyon on Clover Mountain.

"Why are they so intent on kicking us off?" my father asked as we rode. "Your friend Edward Abbey and all his eco-terrorist cohorts. They want us off this slope. They say we're mistreating it. I don't know how they figure. We've been on this allotment ten years. No cow ever set foot on this country until ten years ago. It's in better shape now than it was then. And it's no different than the Upper Well country where cattle have grazed for nearly a century. Rain is the thing that makes the difference. Not cattle."

We came to a giant power line. Steel towers rose fifty feet above us, odd looking metal monsters bearing thick cables carrying megawatts to the gridlocked masses of California. As we rode across the 'dozed area beneath the wires, the buzz from above spooked our horses. They danced over the cleared path, then settled. A little further on Dad noticed the remains of a desert tortoise, its shell turned over and bleaching in the sunshine.

"Coyote," Dad said. "But you won't see that in the reports. They'll say a cow stepped on him. When the shell is upside down like that, it's a coyote kill. Damned coyote ate that turtle right out of house and home."

We rode on. Dad hummed some more. Before long he was talking again. "I wonder if they ever figured the nuclear testing into it," he said. "That radiation is still killing people. Why wouldn't it kill turtles, too?" The desert tortoise weighed heavy on my father's mind. Those crusty old reptiles were crawling, one labored step at a time, to the top of the list. Once they got there, it would be the end. Dad was gathering cows that spring under the strained reality that it might be the last time.

"The good old days are gone," Dad said. "There's more people out there interested in regulating you than helping you make a go of it. Maybe I should have gone to the coast like everyone else. I could have learned to negotiate those freeways. I could have made a lot better living for the family."

"Don't get off on that, Dad," I said. "I see those bumper stickers all the time, the ones that say, 'California Native.' It doesn't seem to me like something you'd necessarily want to advertise."

Dad grinned and sent me on a circle down across a flat where a few brown dots indicated cattle. Twenty minutes later I circled them, six or eight cows with three or four spritely fresh calves. I started them back toward the power line and marveled at the beautiful slick calves. It came to me in a simple thought; I realized then how it must be those calves that keep Dad going year after year—the hope of a new crop of handsome baby calves miraculously appearing every spring. They are products of this desert's stingy vegetation, an amazing variety of grass and plants and brush that would go unused and wither and die and burn in the sun if there weren't a few cows to harvest them. Dad met me an hour later with a dozen head of his own and we trailed them northward toward the corrals. The cows insisted on using the 'dozed pathway where D9 Cats had ripped a fifty-yard-wide swath as far as the eye could see in both directions. They had torn the earth to shreds to make way for the power line. It occurred to me that a thousand cows could not, on their worst behavior, have wreaked this kind of damage in a century of grazing. Rather than fight them, we followed the cows beneath the buzzing wires. Our horses soon settled under the static, reluctantly accepting this new, electrified environment.

"Do you ever think about how lucky you are?" I asked Dad as we rode along behind the cows. "Nowadays everybody wishes they could be a cowboy. You're one of the lucky few."

"One of the final few," Dad said. "I'm afraid we've come to the last generation. We're the only ones left down here."

"You and Uncle Eldon and Afton," I said.

"Yep. And Marv to do the cooking."

"I'll bet people would pay a hundred dollars a day to do this," I said.

"That's what it's coming to," said Dad.

Suddenly I felt an alien force about us. I looked into the sky directly above me and saw a giant craft floating there. It had skulked up from behind, and it was a gruesome, greenish brown mass of molded hardware. It looked like it weighed a thousand tons, and it must have cost more than every cow and every horse and every ranch in all of southern Utah. Hovering so close, maybe five hundred feet above the ground, it seemed extraterrestrial. Silently it hung above us.

Dad looked at me, then up at the air force bomber whose wingspan seemed that of a football field. The jet floated over in eerie silence, making its morning bombing run from Nellis, apparently following the power line north to its target. Quickly behind it trailed the scream. It was an unearthly scream and it shook the rocks. The horses bolted. I could feel the pounding inside my mount and I wondered if he would fall over and die; I'd heard of such things happening. As quickly and mysteriously as it appeared, the bomber and its ghostly scream were gone.

In the new and peaceful silence, Dad gathered his reins and pulled back to the herd. "Do you think they got us?" he asked.

"Yep," I said. "I think we're history."

ᑌ ᗱ ᑌ

...AT SOME POINT
*in the cloudy night a brindle bull—slit in the right ear, crop in the left—
crashes over the summit corral gate and disappears into darkness. From
what Afton can ascertain the next morning, Ol' Brindle has returned to
Burnt Canyon.*

Lyman Hafen is a fifth-generation southern Utahn. He was born and raised in St. George, and spent many summers on the family ranch in Clover Valley, Nevada, where his Mormon pioneer great-great-grandfather settled in the late 1860s. He was the Utah State High School Bareback Bronc Riding Champion and All Around Cowboy in 1973, and was a nationally ranked collegiate rodeo competitor for Dixie College and Brigham Young University, where he graduated in 1979 with a degree in communications.

One of the founding editors of *St. George Magazine*—now in its twelfth year—Hafen has written for numerous regional and national publications, including *Arizona Highways*, *Nevada Magazine*, *Travel Holiday*, *Western Horseman*, and *Northern Lights*. Since 1986, he has been honored seven times by the Utah Arts Council for excellence in writing. His novel for young readers, *Over the Joshua Slope*, was published by Macmillan in 1994.

Hafen has taught writing at Dixie College, is chairman of the Zion Natural History Association, and still ropes in rodeos from time to time. He lives in Santa Clara, Utah, with his wife, Debbie, and five children.